TWAYNE'S WORLD AUTHORS SERIES
A Survey of the World's Literature

Sylvia E. Bowman, Indiana University
GENERAL EDITOR

SPAIN

Gerald Wade, Vanderbilt University
Janet W. Díaz, University of North Carolina at Chapel Hill
EDITORS

Diego de Saavedra Fajardo

TWAS 437

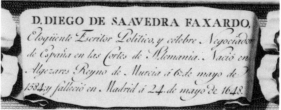

D. DIEGO DE SAAVEDRA FAXARDO,
Eloqüente Escritor Político, y celebre Negociador
de España en las Cortes de Alemania. Nació en
Algezares Reyno de Murcia á 6. de mayo de
1584. y falleció en Madrid á 24. de mayo de 1648.

Diego de Saavedra Fajardo

DIEGO DE SAAVEDRA FAJARDO

By JOHN DOWLING

The University of Georgia

TWAYNE PUBLISHERS

A DIVISION OF G. K. HALL & CO., BOSTON

Copyright©1977 by G. K. Hall & Co.
All Rights Reserved
First Printing

Library of Congress Cataloging in Publication Data

Dowling, John Clarkson, 1920-
  Diego de Saavadra Fajardo.

  (Twayne's world authors series ; TWAS 437 : Spain)
  Bibliography: p. 145 - 57.
  Includes index.
  1. Saavedra Fajardo, Diego de, 1584 - 1648.
2. Authors, Spanish—17th century—Bibliography.
PQ6431.S13Z67   868'.3'09   76-56178
ISBN 0-8057-6200-0

To Robert

Contents

About the Author

John Dowling holds the A. B. degree from the University of Colorado and the A.M. and Ph.D. degrees from the University of Wisconsin. He has been Professor of Spanish and chairman of the department at Texas Tech, Indiana University, and the University of Georgia. He is a Corresponding Member of the Hispanic Society of America. Professor Dowling is the author of *El pensamiento político-filosófico de Saavedra Fajardo,* which was awarded a cash prize by the Academy of Alfonso X the Wise of Murcia, Spain. He is the editor of a Spanish edition of Saavedra Fajardo's *Republic of Letters* and has published several articles dealing with the author and his works.

Professor Dowling is known as well for scholarly works dealing with the Spanish eighteenth century and Romanticism and with the modern Spanish theater. He wrote the Twayne volume on Leandro Fernández de Moratín and is author of a biography of the Spanish Romantic composer, José Melchor Gomis. As a Markham Fellow from the University of Wisconsin, a Guggenheim Fellow, and the recipient of American Philosophical Society and other grants, he has made frequent visits to Spain for research and has published the results in such scholarly journals and reviews as *Hispania, Hispanic Review, Hispanófila, Modern Language Journal, Estreno, The American Hispanist, Insula,* and others.

Preface

Two sixteenth-century dates epitomize the apogee and the nadir of Spanish prestige in the reign of Philip II: 1571 and 1588. On October 7, 1571, the infidel Turks were defeated by the Christian forces of Spain and Venice in a naval battle fought at the entrance to the Gulf of Lepanto in western Greece. It was "the greatest occasion that the past or present has ever known or the future may ever hope to see," wrote Miguel de Cervantes, who in the battle lost the use of his left hand for the greater glory of the right.[1] Seventeen years later, in July of 1588, the Spanish Armada was defeated off the coast of England. Spanish power and prestige did not suddenly disappear, but the first great nation of modern times entered a period of slow decline that was to continue for a century and a half, and accelerate still later.

Diego de Saavedra Fajardo belonged to a generation of writers that was born between those two dates. Preceding them were Cervantes, Lope de Vega, and Góngora; Calderón was to follow. The literary works of this generation that was born between glory and defeat lie at the very core of Spanish Golden Age literature. Saavedra and his contemporaries are the heart of the Spanish Baroque: the poets, Luis Carrillo y Sotomayor, Francisco de Rioja, Pedro Soto de Rojas, the Prince of Esquilache, and the Count of Villamediana; the dramatists, Luis Vélez de Guevara, Juan Ruiz de Alarcón, Tirso de Molina, and Diego Jiménez de Enciso; the novelists, Alonso Jerónimo de Salas Barbadillo, Alonso de Castillo Solórzano, and Gonzalo de Céspedes y Meneses; the sacred orator, Hortensio Paravicino; and the polygraph—the greatest figure of them all—Francisco de Quevedo.

They were a generation born after the Counter-Reformation had taken firm hold on the lives and minds of Spaniards. Against the threats of the Protestant revolt, their country had made a commitment to counterreform and the preservation of the Roman Catholic faith. They grew to manhood and lived out their lives in years made turbulent by this commitment.

They had a number of characteristics in common. They were the most highly schooled of any generation of Spanish writers up to their time. Nearly all of them attended one or more of the universities that flourished in Spain at the turn of the century. In their youth, the court settled permanently in Madrid, and most authors resided at court and did much of their writing there. They traveled less, although Saavedra himself was the exception. Among his contemporaries, Ruiz de Alarcón was born in Mexico, and both Tirso de Molina and the Prince of Esquilache went to the New World in an official capacity. Yet the New World did not beckon strongly, and the development of the closed society of the seventeenth century is already evident in the youth of these men. Saavedra Fajardo, who spent most of his career outside Spain, was unusual in his generation, which contrasts with earlier generations of men who grew up in the glorious years of the Emperor Charles V and Philip II.

In Cervantes's day, several writers wielded both the sword and the pen. Saavedra's generation is noticeably less military. Vélez de Guevara was a soldier, and Luis Carrillo was a naval officer. But most of the authors were trained in civil or canon law, and they worked as priests or as attorneys and secretaries, often in the burgeoning governmental bureaucracy that Philip II had created. Many of them enjoyed the patronage of the Count-Duke of Olivares, and were swept up in the animosities that surrounded him.

This generation contributed enormously to the seventeenth-century outpouring of literary works. In some cases they followed patterns and trends already set. In others, they rejected one direction in order to continue by another path. The drama, firmly established by public approval of the form set for it by Lope, developed within those set limits. In poetry the followers and the opponents of Góngora waged their quarrel with incendiary violence. Although the writers of this generation read *Don Quixote* in their youth, Cervantes had no followers. The picaresque novel took a direction different from that given it by Mateo Alemán, as the moral structure weakened in favor of either inconsequence or verbal humor. On the other hand, moral standards were firmly upheld by an outpouring of didactic literature which continued sixteenth-century trends unabated. The writing of history enjoyed a resurgence which would lead to reforms at the end of the seventeenth century.

By 1648, when the deaths of Tirso de Molina and Saavedra Fajardo followed the passing of Ruiz de Alarcón, Vélez de Guevara, and
Quevedo, the heyday of this generation had passed. The writers had
spent their adult lives within the reigns of the pious Philip III and
the frivolous Philip IV, when the glories of Spain belonged more to
the past than to the present. Their intellectual world was closed,
and they reworked inherited forms. Conceptism triumphed because
they had to express old ideas in a way that would sound new. Thus
Quevedo stands out as a leading light. On the minority side is
Saavedra Fajardo, whose sparkling clarity convinces the reader that
the writer is saying something new and brilliant when he is really
only stating old truths with epigrammatic insight.

No book has presented Saavedra Fajardo to the general public of
the English-speaking world. Some of his works had a vogue in
eighteenth-century England and were translated into English. I
suspect that *República literaria* (*Republic of Letters*) may have influenced Jonathan Swift in an incident in Book III of *Gulliver's
Travels*, when the protagonist visits the island of Glubbdubdrib.[2]
Saavedra has not, however, enjoyed among the English the favor
that they have accorded other Spanish moralists such as Antonio de
Guevara or Baltasar Gracián. Yet Saavedra deserves our attention.
We know the world of the seventeenth century chiefly through the
eyes of the victors in the great struggle that definitively shifted
power, geographically from the Mediterranean and spiritually from
the true faith as Spaniards saw it. Saavedra Fajardo's works permit
us to see the conflict from the point of view of the vanquished.

I have not confined all discussion of Saavedra's life to the initial
biographical section of this book. His works are so clearly a product
of his student and public life and of the times in which he lived that
I have introduced each work with an account of the circumstances
in which it was written.

A word about Diego de Saavedra Fajardo's name may be helpful
for some readers. Diego is his baptismal name. While the particle *de*
suggests that he was of good birth (and he was), it simply indicates
that he was a member of the Saavedra and Fajardo families. He
often omitted it, but it is now traditional to use it with his name. It
should not be used with the surnames unless the baptismal name
precedes it. Saavedra was his father's surname on the paternal side,
while Fajardo was his mother's surname from her father's side. Both
are "strong" surnames; that is, they are not frequent ones like Pérez

or Gómez. In speaking or writing of Diego de Saavedra Fajardo, he may be called by his full name, or Diego de Saavedra, or Saavedra alone (omitting *de*), or Saavedra Fajardo (also omitting *de*). Since both surnames are strong, he should not be called Fajardo alone: no one will understand who he is by that name only.

I first began my studies of Saavedra Fajardo under the influence of several articles by Azorín which I acknowledge in the bibliography. Since then, many have been the scholars and friends who have encouraged me, and hence many the debts I have contracted. I shall name first my former professors at the University of Wisconsin, Everett Hesse and Mark Singleton, who worked with me in the early stages of my research.

Later, in Madrid, I met the excellent critic and beloved man of letters, Juan Guerrero Ruiz, whom Lorca called the "Consul General of Poetry" because of his catalytic influence on contemporary poets.[3] A native Murcian who once lived on the Calle de Saavedra Fajardo in his native city, he gave to me and to my scholarly studies on Saavedra the same vital encouragement that he did to creative writing. On a Sunday morning in 1951, he invited me to accompany Don José Ballester, editor of *La Verdad* in Murcia, for a private visit to the Museo Romántico of Madrid, one of many institutions in which Don Juan took a special interest. During that visit, in those charming salons that have no special connection with Saavedra Fajardo, the two of them inquired about my work with him and urged me to enter a manuscript in the international competition on Saavedra that had recently been announced by the Academy of Alfonso X the Wise of Murcia. Thanks to them, I did so, and the jury awarded my manuscript one of the cash prizes.

I visited Murcia at the time the prizes were awarded and was warmly welcomed by members and friends of the Academy and the University whose good will I enjoyed in the years afterward: Don Felipe González, President of the Academy; Don Agustín Virgili Quintanilla, Director; and Don Eugenio Úbeda Romero, Secretary; Don Mariano Baquero Goyanes, Don Andrés Sobejano Alcayna, Don Antonio Truyol y Serra, and Don Ángel Valbuena Prat, among many others.

In that same competition, another prize—the largest one—was awarded to Don Manuel Fraga Iribarne for his study *Don Diego de Saavedra Fajardo y la diplomacia de su época*, a book superior to mine by far, to which anyone who writes on Saavedra Fajardo must owe a debt. Years later, after Dr. Fraga had been Minister of Information and Tourism and before he served as Spanish Ambassador in London, when he was filling his chair as professor at the University of Madrid, I met him and was able to appreciate that his study of Saavedra had left its mark on his thinking and hence on his public life.

My debt to some of the great scholars of our time is amply attested in the notes and bibliography. To some, however, I must extend special thanks. Professor Otis Green of the University of Pennsylvania, who was as kind as he could be in reviewing my earlier book, has turned his attention to Saavedra from time to time, and his investigations and his insights have always been of great value. Don Enrique Tierno Galván, who served on the jury that rewarded my entry in the Academy competition, has written superb studies, especially on Tacitism, which have helped me greatly in my thinking. Don Juan Antonio Maravall gave me, through his books and articles, an early and much-needed orientation into the vast body of moral, didactic, and political literature of the seventeenth century. In later books and in the conversations we have had in Madrid over a period of years, he has continued his able instruction.

My thanks go to Dr. Francis Very of Northwestern University, whose interest in my work on Saavedra Fajardo has long been a source of encouragement, and to his students Bradley Shaw and Alan Messick. The latter consulted my own collection of works by and about Saavedra; and in turn they provided me with copies of the annotated bibliographies which they prepared as a class project in 1969.

Over the years the grants and fellowships that I have held, even when they were for projects unrelated to Saavedra Fajardo, have given me access to libraries and archives where I have added to my materials about him. The Albert P. Markham Travelling Fellowship from the University of Wisconsin was awarded me especially for studies on Saavedra. A John Simon Guggenheim Fellowship, though specifically for my studies on Moratín, resulted in discoveries that have enriched my Saavedra text. An award from the American Philosophical Society enabled me to bring to completion a complicated bibliographical study of *República literaria* (*Republic of Letters*); and small grants from Texas Tech University, Indiana

University, and the University of Georgia have supported my research. To all of these institutions I acknowledge a debt of gratitude.

JOHN DOWLING

The University of Georgia

Chronology

1584   May 6. Diego de Saavedra Fajardo, born on the family estate near Murcia, was baptized in the parochial church of Santa María de Loreto in Algezares.

1600   He began his studies in jurisprudence and canon law at the University of Salamanca.

1606   April 21. He took his bachelor's degree in canon law at Salamanca. Then he went to Rome to begin a public career spanning thirty-four years in the principal courts of Europe.

ca. 1608   He became associated, as legal or executive secretary, with Don Gaspar de Borja y Velasco, younger brother of the Duke of Gandía and member of the family known in Italy as the Borgias.

1611   August 17. Gaspar de Borja received his cardinal's hat.

1611-
1612   Saavedra contributed poems to two books, one published in Barcelona and Madrid, the other in Rome.

1612   A manuscript of his *República literaria* (*Republic of Letters*) is dated this year.

1614   He contributed a Latin epigram to *Tablas poéticas* (*Poetic Tables*), published in Murica by his former teacher Francisco Cascales.

1615-
1620   Concurrently with his post as secretary to Cardinal Borja, he handled the affairs of the Kingdom of Naples and Sicily in Rome.

1616-
1619   Assuming additional duties, Saavedra served as secretary of the Spanish Embassy in Rome while Cardinal Borja was ambassador.

1617   July 23. Saavedra was appointed a canon of the cathedral of Santiago de Compostela, a post he held until 1621. He did not reside there but handled cathedral business in Rome.

1620   May-December. Borja served as interim Viceroy of Naples, and Saavedra acted as his Secretary of State and War.

1621   As secretary to Cardinal Borja, Saavedra attended the conclave at which Gregory XV was elected Pope.

1623   Again as Borja's secretary, he attended the conclave at which Urban VIII was elected Pope.

1623-   He served Philip IV as head of his General Agency in
1633   Rome with the title of Procurator and Solicitor General for Castile and the Indies.

1630   December 29. In Madrid he dated an essay in Italian entitled *Indisposizione generale della monarchia di Spagna: sue cause e remedii* (*General Malady of the Spanish Monarchy: Its Causes and Cures*).

1631   February 1. He presented the Count-Duke of Olivares with an incomplete draft of *Introducciones a la política* (*Introduction to Political Science*) and *Razón de Estado del Rey Católico Don Fernando* (*Statecraft of King Ferdinand the Catholic*).

1631-   He again served as secretary of the Spanish Embassy in
1633   Rome while Borja was ambassador.

1633-   Chosen as minister to the court of Maximilian of Bav-
1642   aria, he served the Spanish cause in central Europe for a decade, residing normally in Munich but traveling over the entire area during the final phases of the Thirty Years' War.

1635   In reply to France's declaration of war against Spain on June 6, Saavedra published his *Respuesta al manifiesto de Francia* (*Answer to the French Declaration*), pretending to be a French gentleman writing to his king.

1636   December. Saavedra attended the Electoral College at Regensburg which chose Ferdinand III, King of Hungary and Bohemia and Archduke of Austria, as Holy Roman Emperor.

1637   January 20. In Regensburg he composed *Discurso sobre el estado presente de Europa* (*Discourse on the Present State of Europe*), which he sent to the Cardinal-Infante Fernando and Philip IV.

1638   March-April. He negotiated treaties with the Duchess of Mantua.

1638   Pretending to be a Swiss, he wrote *Dispertador a los trece cantones de esguízaros* (*Warning to the Thirteen Swiss Cantons*).

1638   June-July. As representative of the Spanish crown, he went on a peace mission to Franche-Comté, and

	reported it in *Relación de la jornada al condado de Borgoña* (*A Journey to the County of Burgundy*).
1638-1642	As ambassador plenipotentiary to the Swiss cantons, he attended meetings of eight Diets.
1639	February 27. Saavedra presented, in Italian, his *Proposta fatta dal Sig. Don Diego Sciavedra alla Dieta de cantoni catolici in Lucerna* (*Proposal Made by Don Diego Saavedra to the Diet of Catholic Cantons in Lucerne*).
1640	July 10. In Vienna Saavedra signed the dedication of *Idea de un príncipe político-cristiano* (*Concept of a Political-Christian Prince*), which was translated into English in 1700 with the title *The Royal Politician*. The book, also called by its shortened subtitle, *Cien Empresas* (*One Hundred Essays*), or *Empresas políticas* (*Political Essays*), came out in Munich before the end of the year.
1640	September 18. Philip IV granted Saavedra membership as a knight in the Order of St. James.
1640-1641	He attended the Imperial Diet in Regensburg, and discussed possible peace negotiations between the Empire and France and Sweden.
1640-1643	Before this period he revised *Republic of Letters*, and sometime during it he wrote the dedication to the Count-Duke of Olivares.
1643	January 19. Back in Madrid, he took possession of his post as a member of the Council of Indies, to which he had been appointed in 1635.
1643	Between January and March (fall of Olivares and death of Louis XIII of France), he wrote the tract *Suspiros de Francia* (*Sighs of France*).
1643	July 11. He was named minister plenipotentiary to the Peace Congress at Münster, province of Westphalia, where he stayed until the end of 1645.
1643 or 1644	He composed *Locuras de Europa* (*Folly of Europe*), of which no printed edition is known until 1748.
1645	September 8. He dated the dedication of *Corona gótica* (*Gothic Crown*) at Münster, where it was published in 1646.
1646-1648	He served in Madrid as a member of the Council of Indies.
1648	August 24. Saavedra died in Madrid.

CHAPTER 1

The Republic of Letters

IN 1592, when the boy Diego de Saavedra Fajardo was eight years old, Don Sancho Dávila, bishop of Cartagena, opened a seminary in Murcia, named for St. Fulgentius of Ruspe and dedicated to training youths for the priesthood. It has been surmised that Diego, a younger son of a distinguished family, attended this school.[1] These early years, however, are visible to us as through a mist. Diego appears to have known, possibly in Cartagena or perhaps in Murcia, a boy a year his senior, Luis Carrillo y Sotomayor (1583 - 1610), who was to distinguish himself as a cultist poet.[2] He was also a friend of Alonso Cano y Urreta, later the author of *Días del jardín* (*Days in the Garden;* Madrid, 1619). While Cano's title does not suggest the contents, the book dealt with subjects close to Saavedra's adult interests, including the refutation of Machiavellianism and the problems of statecraft—called "razón de Estado" in the famous Spanish phrase.[3]

It is probable that Diego studied with Francisco Cascales (1567? - 1642) before the humanist left Murcia in 1597 to teach in Cartagena. In 1601 Cascales was back teaching at the Seminary of St. Fulgentius, but by then Diego had gone to Salamanca. Cascales wrote, in dialogue, *Tablas poéticas* (*Principles of Poetics*), in which he adapted Greco-Roman literary ideas to Renaissance tastes. He had finished the book as early as 1614, but it went unpublished until his young friend, Saavedra Fajardo, in Rome in 1614, called the work to the attention of Fernando de Castro, Count of Castro, and at the time Viceroy of Sicily. With the financial aid of this distinguished magnate, the book appeared in print in 1617.[4]

With notions of literature that must have been basically classical, young Diego de Saavedra Fajardo left the banks of Murcia's Segura River for the banks of the River Tormes. In 1600, as the Baroque age opened in Spanish literature and art, he crossed Spain to matriculate in the University of Salamanca. He was sixteen when he arrived, and he remained there until he was at least twenty-two. He may have stayed until 1608, for it is uncertain whether his two years as a teaching assistant were concurrent with his undergraduate studies or followed the awarding of his bachelor's degree.

I   *The Golden City*

By 1600 Salamanca, both the city and the University, had a rich tradition of history, literature, and art. Although in Roman times it was comparatively a minor town, it was situated on the main north-south route of Hispania Ulterior between Betica and Galicia. The Romans built an arched bridge over the Tormes River, which gave access to the city from the south, as it still does today.

When young Diego crossed the bridge in 1600, he must have been impressed by the old cathedral and the nearby buildings which were constructed of a golden sandstone. Silhouetted against the blue Iberian sky, they gave a warm glow to the city. The old cathedral, Santa María de la Sede, dated its foundations from the beginning of the twelfth century, and its dome—called the Cock's Tower because of the weathervane on top—is thought to have been finished before the end of that century. Its chapels had been the first classrooms of the University, and in 1600 they were still used for certain academic functions. For example, in the Santa Barbara Chapel the professors conducted examinations for the doctorate. The candidate sat in a stone armchair at the foot of the founder's tomb while the professors ranged themselves in seats along the walls from where they bombarded their victim with questions. Some examinations were said to have lasted a full twenty-four hours. If a candidate was successful, he was obliged to pay for a celebration that began with a banquet in the nearby Chapel of Santa Catalina. A bullfight was required, and with the blood of the bull the new doctor wrote his name on the walls of the church (and later on the University buildings) followed by the word "Victor," the letters of which were arranged in an imaginative design. The banquet and the bullfight are not required today, but the modern Ph.D. still paints his name and "Victor" in red ocher on the walls.

The new cathedral, which stands beside and even encroaches on the old one, belongs to the flamboyant Gothic style. It was begun less than ninety years before young Diego arrived in Salamanca and was still abuilding, for it was not consecrated until 1733. Its golden sandstone, like that of the older buildings, was quarried from the valley of the Tormes, both upstream and downstream from the city, where sediment of sand, red clay, and oxide of iron mingled to impart a distinctive color to the stone. Soft when taken from the quarries, it hardened when it dried; as the stone weathered, oxidation gave it the luminous golden hue that characterizes Salamanca.

Near the two cathedrals were the University buildings that were constructed when enrollment outgrew the chapels of the old cathedral. The Escuelas Mayores, or Major Schools, were begun in 1415. The magnificent west façade of the school building was not finished until more than a century later, and represents the peak of Plateresque art. On it, a bas-relief medallion with portraits of Ferdinand and Isabel commemorated the attention which the Catholic sovereigns lavished on Salamanca. An inscription, in Greek, is the motto of their age: "The beginning of wisdom is the fear of God."

The patios and rooms of the interior harmonize the Gothic, Mudéjar, and Plateresque styles which prevailed in Spanish architecture in the 120-year period during which the halls were built. Everywhere there is evidence of the endeavor to provide a fit setting for the education of Spain's elite. Above the door of the classroom (today named for the music professor Francisco de Salinas, 1513 - 1590) in which Diego de Saavedra studied civil law is this statement in Latin: "In this classroom the University Council endeavored to instruct youth in the knowledge of their elders that princes might govern well their states and justly resolve disputes among men so that peace and justice might reign in the hearts of all."[5]

In the theology classroom students stood or sat on the floor until Francisco de Vitoria (1486 - 1546), theologian and pioneer of international jurisprudence, brought about installation of desks made of split logs. By Saavedra Fajardo's time, this rough furniture was already carved with the names or initials of students who had heard there the lectures of Fray Luis de Léon (1527? - 1591), the ascetic poet and theologian. Canon law, in which Diego de Saavedra majored, was taught in a handsomely vaulted room that serves as the assembly hall for ceremonies and "solemn acts" of the University.

The chapel, which had once housed the library, dated from the second half of the fifteenth century. In Saavedra's time the ceiling was decorated with a painting by Fernando Gallegos with forty-eight images of the eighth sphere of heaven depicting the winds, the symbols of the constellations, and the astrological signs. (What remains of the painting may be seen today in a room in the Escuelas Menores, the Minor Schools.) The *retablo* (altarpiece) was by Juan de Flandes, and Juan de Borgoña had done paintings of the Annunciation and the Adoration of the Magi.

In the chapel tower was an elaborate clock. An image of a black man struck the great bell to give the hours. Two battering rams marked the half-hour by alternately butting the bell. At 9:00 A.M. statues of the three Wise Men and of two angels knelt before an image of the Virgin Mary at the crèche. The clock even showed the phases of the moon so that night-wandering students might know what moonlight they could expect.

The Plateresque sculptures which decorated the staircase that led to the upper cloister must have diverted student eyes with their piquant humor: along the first flight jongleurs and maids dance amidst floral decoration; along the second, nude men and women cavort and ride astride other men and women likewise nude.

The library, located on the second floor, was rich both in the decoration of its quarters and in its holdings. Professors and friends of the University had lavished attention on it. An anteroom to the library proper possessed an extraordinary Moorish ceiling carved of chestnut wood. A Gothic arch, fitted with a Renaissance grillwork of intricate design, gave access to the library. Thousands of manuscripts had accumulated since Alfonso X the Wise had created in 1254 the first state-supported library with a salaried librarian. To them had been added a growing collection of printed books of the end of the fifteenth century and the whole of the sixteenth.

The work of the University was also carried on in the Minor Schools, in the Trilingual College which taught Hebrew, Greek, and Latin, as well as rhetoric and the humanities, and in the many residential colleges located throughout the city. At the entrance to the Minor Schools, a shield of the University, placed there in the early, optimistic years of the sixteenth century, is half encircled by a Latin inscription that boasts: "Salamanca is first in the teaching of all knowledge."[6]

From these halls came the men who administered the empire that had been won by men of action like Hernán Cortés and by unlettered men like Francisco Pizarro. Graduates in theology carried the word of God, of the Virgin, and of Christ to the Indies and to the Orient. Men of Salamanca were employed in the world's first great bureaucracy created by Philip II. The best, the elite like Saavedra Fajardo, graduated from the "republic of letters" to enter the diplomatic service of His Most Catholic Majesty—the Spanish monarch—who, in the seventeenth century, was pitted against His Most Christian Majesty—the French monarch—in a struggle for

European power. Most of Saavedra's life and work were to be governed by that struggle, but those problems did not yet exist for him at Salamanca. He could devote himself to the learning that is apparent in his first book, *República literaria (Republic of Letters)*.

The city was steeped in literary memories. Local tradition insists that the Bachelor Fernando de Rojas chose Salamanca as the setting for his dialogue novel *La tragicomedia de Calisto y Melibea (The Tragicomedy of Calisto and Melibea)*, better known as the *Celestina* after one of the most fascinating characters in Spanish literature.[7] Although Toledo might dispute the claim, Salamancan legend located the house of this bawd and go-between, Mother Celestina, not far from the student quarter near the banks of the River Tormes. It was easy to imagine, in a better part of the city, the garden in which Calisto and Melibea first met, the wall he scaled clandestinely to seduce her and from which he fell to his death, the tower from which the distraught Melibea cast herself to die at her father's feet.

Other literary traditions are more certain. Juan del Encina, father of the Spanish drama, had brought portrayals of rustic life in the province of Salamanca to noble halls in his short dialect plays. One of them, the *Auto del repelón (Brawling Scene)*, relates a clash between students of Salamanca and country shepherds.

In the Tormes River itself, the pícaro Lazarillo—creation of an anonymous author—was born, so he says, because his mother was beset with labor pains while at her husband's flour mill. In Salamanca the boy was employed by his first master, the blind man. At the Roman bridge the old man played a mean trick on the boy. He told Lazarillo to put his ear to the primitive statue of a bull and he would hear a noise inside. When Lazarillo did as he was told, the sadistic old man boxed his head against the bull's head and laughed at his own trick, telling the pained child that a blind man's boy ought to be sharper than the devil himself. The statue was there in Saavedra's time as it still is today.

St. Teresa de Jésus (1515 - 1582), who one day would be a doctor *honoris causa* of the University, arrived in Salamanca in early November of 1570, and stopped at a dilapidated fifteenth-century mansion located on a plaza that now bears her name. There the founder of Discalced Carmelite convents and her companion Sister Isabel spent the eve of All Souls, without furniture, sleeping on the second floor in some straw. In 1571, St. Teresa experienced an ecstatic trance in the same house which she was then rebuilding, and there she wrote her famed poem "Vivo sin vivir en mí. . . ."

(I have an existence—in Christ—which is beyond myself, she means to say.) A few miles out of town, on the road to Alba de Tormes, was the fountain from which the saint drank on her trips back and forth, and in Alba itself her incorrupt body lay in the Carmelite convent that she had founded.

In 1600 the University of Salamanca was steeped in 350 years of tradition. Alcalá de Henares, its nearest rival in quality, was barely a century old. Surely there was no better place in the peninsula for a bright young man than the republic of letters on the banks of the Tormes.

II Students from Salamanca

"Everything has its beginning, its peak, and its decline." The idea appears repeatedly in Saavedra Fajardo's works. Before he arrived in Salamanca, the University had attained its greatest splendor. Don Diego was a student there in the period when it began its long descent into decadence.

Founded in 1243 in the reign of Fernando III, the saint, Salamanca was Spain's great medieval university; it ranked with Paris, Oxford, and Bologna. Cardinal Jiménez de Cisneros established the University of Alcalá de Henares at the beginning of the sixteenth century and contributed a powerful new force to the Spanish Renaissance. During the sixteenth century minor universities functioned even in improbable towns—Osuna, for example—and were often the butt of mockery. In 1600 the distinguished universities were still Salamanca for its age and tradition and Alcalá de Henares for its modernity and dynamism.

In Cervantes's novel *El ingenioso hidalgo Don Quijote de la Mancha* (*The Ingenious Gentleman Don Quixote de la Mancha*), the first part of which was published in 1605 while Saavedra Fajardo was a student, and the second in 1615, a few years after he left the University, we meet several students from Salamanca. One is Sansón Carrasco, a Bachelor of Arts. At the beginning of the second part of the novel, he returns home to the village in La Mancha while Don Quixote and Sancho Panza are recovering from the adventures of the knight's second sortie. Sancho Panza brings his master an astounding piece of news which the B.A. from Salamanca, who keeps up on literary matters, has just given him: the two of them, master and servant, Don Quixote and Sancho Panza, are the subject of a book that has come out *in print*, written by a Moor named, according to Sancho, Cide Hamete Berenjena (II, ii, 525).[8]

The squire believes young Carrasco, for, as he says later, he "is a bachelor from Salamanca, and people like him can't lie, unless the fancy happens to strike them or they find it very convenient to do so" (II, xxxiii, 733). Sansón likewise has a good opinion of himself. He brushed aside an objection of Don Quixote's housekeeper, telling her, "Don't dispute my word. You know I am a bachelor from Salamanca, and that means the best there is" (II, vii, 550). A group of farmers loitering at a tavern door express their admiration for Sancho's peasant wisdom, and one of them comments: "If the servant is so wise, what must the master be? I'll wager that if they are going to Salamanca to study, they'll become court judges in no time at all" (II, lxvi, 945).

A young man could learn a lot in Salamanca, though it might not avail him much when he fell in love. Grisóstomo, son of a well-to-do gentleman, had spent "many years" as a student in Salamanca whence he returned to his native La Mancha with a reputation for being learned and well-read. He knew the science of the stars and could predict eclipses of the sun and moon. His knowledge of astronomy merged into astrology. He predicted whether the year would be plentiful or sterile, and advised his father and his friends what crops to sow. He had also become something of a poet at Salamanca, and he gave expression to his unrequited passion for the disdainful Marcela in a "Song of Despair," composed in hendeca-syllables with a complicated rhyme scheme (I, xii - xiv).

Poetry became the principal preoccupation of another Salamanca student to the chagrin of his father. Don Diego de Miranda—the gentleman in the green coat—sent his son to the University for six years where he studied the Greek and Latin languages ("the first step on the stairway of learning . . . is that of languages," Don Quixote commented). At the end of that time Don Diego wanted his son to study for a career in law or theology. But young Lorenzo was so immersed in poetry that he took no interest in his father's design. Home on vacation, he spent the whole day trying to decide whether a verse in Homer's *Iliad* was well conceived or not, whether Martial was immodest in a particular epigram, or whether certain lines of Virgil were to be understood in one way or another. He disdained modern Spanish poets; yet he racked his brain to compose a gloss on a quatrain that was sent him from Salamanca so that he might take part in a literary contest (II, xvi, 608).

Less edifying skills than versification could be learned in Salamanca. Don Quixote fell in with two graduates of that distinguished institution on their way to the wedding of the rich young man

Camacho. In their baggage they carried fencing foils. One of them, a licentiate, boasted that he had studied canon law and prided himself on being able to express himself plainly and intelligibly. His companion, the Bachelor Corchuelo, chided him sharply saying that had he devoted as much time to his studies as he had to fencing, he would not have graduated at the tail end of his class. These were fighting words, and the two fell to duelling with foils. The licentiate demonstrated that whatever his skill with the Spanish language, Salamanca had taught him to fence, for he left his antagonist's cassock in shreds (II, xix).

Although the University of Salamanca still preserved an aura of glory in 1600, it had nevertheless begun a decline which, despite eighteenth-century reforms, was not effectively reversed until the rectorship of Miguel de Unamuno in the twentieth century. The turning point had come a generation before Diego de Saavedra Fajardo was born. With the accession of Philip II to the throne in 1559, the doors of Spain began to close, so that Saavedra Fajardo grew up in an increasingly closed society as the monarch fought off incursions of the heresy that Martin Luther had launched in 1517. Spanish students were called home from abroad, and others were permitted to go only to selected institutions. In Spanish universities chairs fell vacant in certain disciplines and were not filled. Although the astronomy of Copernicus had been taught at the University of Salamanca, by the end of the century the chair of astronomy as well as the chairs of physics, mathematics, and natural philosophy, and also other branches of learning were often vacant or occupied by nonentities.

Literature and theology did not disappear from the curriculum, but they never recovered from the accusations of heresy which a petty retired professor of grammar, León de Castro, made against Fray Luis de León and others in the 1570's. Fray Luis de León, a brilliant poet and theologian, had been elected to a chair at Salamanca at the age of thirty-four. Castro and a colleague accused him of uttering dangerous theological propositions, of questioning the accuracy of the Vulgate translation, of preferring the Hebrew text to the Latin, and of translating the Song of Songs as if it were a profane love song. Fray Luis was arrested in 1572 and spent more than four years in the Inquisition's prison in Valladolid. He was eventually tried, sentenced to a reprimand and a retraction of his propositions, and was released in December of 1576. Famous are the words with which he began his first lecture on returning to his classroom at Salamanca: "As I was saying the other day . . . . ."

Fray Luis's colleagues were not so fortunate. One died in prison. Another was freed but did not regain his post. Nor was León de Castro's insidious tongue stilled. He murmured against the Hebrew scholar and humanist Benito Arias Montano, who was publishing the Royal Polyglot Bible in Antwerp. Arias was in Rome, fortunately, far from the Spanish Inquisition's prisons. In 1584, the year Saavedra Fajardo was born, Francisco Sánchez, known as "el Brocense" after his native town Las Brozas, professor of grammar at Salamanca and distinguished man of letters, was denounced for propositions and was reprimanded. He did not take the warning seriously, and at the age of eighty-seven, the old scholar was put under house arrest by the Holy Office.

Fear took its toll. The historian Juan de Mariana, writing in his *History of Spain* published between 1592 and 1605, that is, just before and during Saavedra Fajardo's student days, speaks of the depressed spirits of those professors who saw "how much affliction threatened those who spoke freely what they thought." Thus it came about that the professors agreed readily with currently acceptable ideas and "entertained opinions that were approved of and were the least dangerous, without any great concern for the truth."[9]

Inner erosion was not outwardly evident. Enrollment was at a peak. At the end of the sixteenth century between seven and eight thousand paying students were studying at the University besides friars, canons, and other clerics who enrolled free. In the student body were the sons of dukes, marquesses, and other nobles. Students came from every province in Spain and from Portugal, Mallorca, the Indies, New Spain, and Peru. There were always students from France, Flanders, Italy, England, and Ireland.

The same year, 1600, that Saavedra matriculated at Salamanca, a young Mexican, some three years his senior, enrolled in the fifth course in canon law. Juan Ruiz de Alarcón had begun his studies at the Royal Pontifical University of Mexico and had transferred to Salamanca. There he remained until 1605 when he completed the licentiate in both civil and canon law.[10] Later, from 1616 to 1634, he wrote for the Spanish stage and published plays that earned him a place in the quadrumvirate of the Spanish Golden Age theater along with Lope de Vega, Tirso de Molina, and Calderón de la Barca.

Although the study of letters and of science was in decline, Salamanca was at its peak of opulence. The merchants in Mercaderes Street sold beds and furniture at exorbitant prices to newly arrived students, and when the youths left bought them back cheap.

The owners of the clothing stores in Roperos Street enriched themselves with the sale of showy garments which appealed to student tastes. To provide food for hungry youths, meat, fish, poultry, fruits, and vegetables came to Salamanca from Béjar, Toro, Vera de Plasencia, and more distant points.

In a report on the University made by Diego de Simancas, Bishop of Ciudad Rodrigo, the prelate commented on the expensive way of life of the students: "Their clothes are so magnificent and costly that their estates are insufficient to sustain them. In their apartments they have great beds, tapestries, writing desks, oak tables, and chairs. They wear costly cassocks, cloaks, both everyday and fine soutanes, ridiculous caps with four outsized corners and an opening so small that the cap sits on top of the head, mantles so long that they drag on the ground, and a lot of other foolish stuff of this sort."[11]

III   The Vision

A student could still learn much at Salamanca, and *Republic of Letters* is evidence of what Saavedra Fajardo got out of his studies there. The critic Azorín has said that the book gives us the measure of the education of a cultivated young man in the first years of the seventeenth century.[12] Saavedra relates his narrative as a "vision" after the manner of Lucian or of Plato in *The Republic*. He supposes that he falls asleep and dreams that he finds himself "in sight of a city whose capitals of silver and radiant gold dazzled me with their lustre. . . ." We imagine a city like Salamanca as a brilliant, oblique sun strikes its golden stones. The author continues: "I was captivated with its beauty and had a longing desire to approach it."[13]

A guide appears as if conjured by the young man's wish. He is elderly, his name is Marcus Varro, and the youth—let us call him Saavedra, since he is the author's persona—was acquainted with him through the description of Cicero. Varro (116 - 27 B.C.), a praetor who fought as a partisan of Pompey in Spain, became a librarian and, after experiencing the turmoil of civil war, was able to devote himself to study. He is supposed to have edited almost five hundred books, so that he was indeed an appropriate guide to a city devoted to writing. Today we know the titles of fifty of his works and possess but two of them: *De Lingua Latina* (*On the Latin Language*) in part, and *Rerum Rusticarum Libri III* (*Three Books on Agriculture*).

In the course of the narrative, and unexpectedly for the reader,

Polydore Vergil (1470 - 1555?) substitutes for Varro Vergil's *De Inventoribus Rerum Libri VIII* (*Eight Books on the Inventors of Things;* 1499), which he published before he went to England as a subcollector of Peter's pence, became a sixteenth-century source book of curious information. Just a year after Saavedra Fajardo graduated from Salamanca, Juan de la Cueva (1550? - 1610?) better known as a dramatist, published his Spanish version, *Los inventores de las cosas.* Again unexpectedly Polydore becomes Apollodorus. The intrusion of the Greek grammarian is probably due to a manuscript error, for this guide is metamorphosed once again into Marcus Varro.

At the beginning of the narrative, the youth and the old gentleman strike up a conversation, and Varro offers to show Saavedra the most curious sights of the shining city, which he says is called the Republic of Letters. They approach through fields of hellebore, an herb much in demand among the inhabitants of the city. They thought they were taking it as a specific to improve the memory, but the truth was that their hard studies and lucubrations made them subject to distemper of the brain.

The city was surrounded by a moat filled with ink. The walls were planted with quills. The principal manufactured product was paper. The city gate had columns of marble and jasper; in niches between them stood statues of the nine Muses and of Apollo. Passing through the suburbs which were devoted to the mechanical arts, the pair cross over a gentle river on a marble bridge. Going from portico to portico, they observe men engaged in the fine arts: architects, silversmiths, painters, tapestry weavers, sculptors. Two painters quarrel because each endeavors to outdo the other with *trompe l'oeil* techniques. Another painter, despairing that he cannot imitate the froth on a dog's mouth throws a sponge at his painting, and chance succeeds in portraying the froth where endeavor had not. They witness another dispute between painters and sculptors over which of the arts has primacy. The dispute is settled by Michelangelo himself who proves to them that sculpture, painting, and architecture are equally important and that each one assists the other two.

Varro takes Saavedra to another gate which leads into the city proper. It is adorned with an arch and with figures representing the seven liberal arts and sciences: grammar, logic, rhetoric, arithmetic, music, geometry, and astronomy. It is at this point that Polydore Vergil becomes the youth's guide. Before they pass through the gate, he shows Saavedra and explains to him a sculptured allegory on the invention of printing. As they enter, they see portraits of the inventors of the letters of the alphabet, but before they can advance, they must placate two supercilious grammarians, bearded men loaded down with satchels and bunches of keys, whose intolerable arrogance would have cowed a less curious youth than Saavedra.

The sight that met his eyes on the other side was a fine edifice and before it a great quadrangle which was the scene of feverish activity. They were at the customhouse where books were sent from all over the world. Some carts hauled but a single book, and even so the panting mules were covered with sweat. "So insupportable a load is stupidity," reflected Saavedra, "as to make the very sides of a mule crack to bear it" (p. 37). Numbers of censors were engaged in inspecting books to determine which might circulate in the Republic of Letters, and they rejected more than they passed. The censor of law books was heard to wish that swarms of Goths might again be unleashed to put a stop to the inundation of books. Exhausted by his work load, he contributed books "by the gross to light fires with, and to put fish or hog's lard in" (p. 39).

The censor of creative literature disposed of unwanted books quaintly. Amorous works might be used to wrap candy, while satirical literature was to be used for pepper or snuff. Other censors thought of similar, picturesquely appropriate means of disposing of unwanted works. History books were to be cut into triumphal arches and festoons. Books on physics were used as wads for guns. However, political treatises were consigned directly to the flames because they contained so much venom.

Escaping from the hurly-burly of the quadrangle, Saavedra the character entered the customhouse and found himself in a hall with a ceiling painted like the one by Fernando Gallegos that Saavedra the student had seen in the chapel at the University of Salamanca:

Upon the roof of the hall was drawn all the brightness of the eighth sphere with the several constellations, the zodiac adorned with its twelve signs intersecting the sphere, and from the four corners upon which this circle was drawn, there rushed forth the four winds. The east wind came forth wrapped in white clouds; the west, ruddy and turbulent; the south wind breathed out flowers; and the north shook out of his gloomy mantle snow and hail. Upon the four sides described the seasons of the year. The spring was crowned with roses; the summer showed herself decked with ears of corn; autumn with vine leaves; and winter appeared covered with dry and parched up brambles (pp. 45 - 46).

Beneath this painting was a balance in which "men's talents were weighed by the pound and ounce, but their judgments only by drams and scruples" (pp. 46 - 47). Saavedra recognized the man in charge, the Sevillian poet Fernando de Herrera (1534 - 97), whose poetry represented the last flowering of Renaissance classicism before the triumph of the Baroque mode. In response to Saavedra's query about the quality of modern poetry, Herrera gave him a discourse on Italian and Spanish poets from Petrarch to Lope de Vega. After this lesson, and while Saavedra watched Antonio de Nebrija and other grammarians instructing aspiring immigrants in the rules of grammar, Polydore Vergil vanished and Marcus Varro was again at Saavedra's side. Commenting on the amount of time spent in learning Latin, Varro attributes the problem to the neglect of parents: "they don't take advantage of the younger years of their children when they are aptest and best disposed by nature for learning languages . . ." (p. 60).

Saavedra witnessed a solemn procession of historians, and now it was Polydore, again at his elbow, who commented on each writer as he passed: Thucydides, Polybius, Plutarch, Xenophon, Sallust, Tacitus, Livy, Suetonius, and Julius Caesar, among the ancients. Among the moderns they saw Philippe de Comines, Guicciardini, Paulo Giovio, Jerónimo Zurita, Diego de Mendoza, and Juan de Mariana. After passing by several libraries and visiting a vale peopled by characters from mythology, Saavedra encountered Socrates and Plato beside a pleasant stream, and a little above them a group of skeptic philosophers. In another quarter were the dogmatists, and moving about were the peripatetics. Stoics, Pythagoreans, Epicureans, Cynics, and Heliacs peopled this garden of philosophy. Reposing apart upon the mossy banks of a stream was Diogenes, "the most disabused and clear-sighted of them all" (p. 85).

Dubiously, Saavedra ventured with Marcus Varro into a cave where they first encountered Artemidorus Daldianus, the Greek soothsayer and interpreter of dreams, and Geronimo Cardano, the Italian mathematician, physician, and astrologer. The latter gave them a disquisition on sleep and dreams before they descended farther into the depths. In the bowels of the earth they found the alchemists, their ragged clothes tattered and scorched, their bodies blackened with smoke. The visitors pitied these creatures and their vain pretensions, for, "in order to make gold, such was their folly, they flung away the little they had . . . ." (p. 93.)

In this nether world they encountered sybils, necromancers, and other soothsayers who each sought to tell the future by means of his specialization: pyromancers (fire), hydromancers (water), sycomancers (leaves), geomancers (dots on the ground), and chiromancers (lines on the hand). The visitors thought it prudent to keep their distance from these creatures and did not speak to them. Issuing from those melancholy depths, the two were dazzled by a view of Mt. Helicon, abode of the Muses, forested with myrtles and laurels. At its base was the Aganippe spring from which flowed the crystalline water of poetic inspiration. On the banks of the silver stream and in the nearby meadows, they saw the great men of letters of ancient and modern times, from Homer and Virgil to Tasso, Camões, and Milton, and many figures of lesser stature. They made a detour to avoid the darts cast at passersby by the satirists Juvenal, Persius, Martial, and Luis de Góngora.

When at last Saavedra entered the city proper, the expectations he had had from its outward appearance were dashed:

The buildings were raised upon false bottoms, and the inhabitants revealed more vanity than judgment. Some seemingly new houses were but old ones newly done up or built out of the ruins of others. This made the city look as if it were turned upside down and in a confusion. The inhabitants were vainly employing their pains upon old repairs and refitting decayed buildings which did not enlarge or add to the luster of the republic but rather lessened and deprived it of those improvements which it would have had if its members had set their heads to work in projecting new plans and models for palaces or public buildings. The people had a melancholy appearance; they were thin-jawed and stupid looking. They were continually at odds, envying and maligning one another. The chief citizens, to be sure, since they had carried the arts and sciences to the greatest height, cut a better figure, and were held in great honor and esteem. But other inferior sorts added only to the bulk of the populace and served to increase the ranks of the vulgar, each applying himself to that calling or business which best suited his profession. . . . In this Republic . . . it was accounted praiseworthy to steal under the pretense of imitation (pp. 103 - 8).

Saavedra stood aside as Maecenas came down one of the streets, lolling in a litter carried by eight slaves. He saw Apuleius pass through the city, too, riding an ass, followed by hundreds of people, some hissing him and others calling him a thief. He admired a magnificent edifice which he was told was the madhouse, "designed rather for the distinction of fools and madmen than for their cure" (p. 112). Inwardly he reflected that a madhouse was "entirely needless in a community which itself might pass very well for such a place" (p. 112). Everything Saavedra learned of the city and ex-

perienced there—the mediocrity, the pettiness, the false-
ness—dampened the enthusiasm with which he entered. Nothing
could be more disheartening than the long harangue which
Democritus gave the visitor. When Saavedra encountered him, the
philosopher was so overcome by immoderate laughter that the
visitor inquired of him the reason: "So many things are there in this
Republic, each one of which would make you die of laughter, be
you ever so melancholy, that only a stranger can be excused for ask-
ing the question" (p. 135).

Democritus then launched a tirade against the folly and vanity of
men of knowledge and letters, against the very disciplines themselves. He mocked writers who dedicate their works to powerful
men who know nothing of the subject treated; the learned ig-
noramuses, insolent with their knowledge of one field, who presume
to opine authoritatively on all subjects; historians who write history
according to their prejudices instead of the facts, yet expect princes
and rulers to follow the precepts that they falsely lay down;
philosophers whose logic is confused by their sophistry; lawyers who
thrive on the quarrels of others; doctors whose insufficiency in their
art is demonstrated if we "observe how few men die natural
deaths. . . . " (p. 163).

The laughing philosopher made fun of the disciplines as well as
of their practitioners. Arithmetic, he says, was born of gambling and
thrives on avarice. While geometry can boast of certain constant
principles, astronomy has given rise to as many opinions as there are
astronomers; yet astrology, based on such uncertain principles,
dares to presage future events. The antidote to Democritus's sar-
donic laughter is provided when Saavedra meets Heraclitus, the
weeping philosopher. His view of the arts and sciences is less cor-
rosively pessimistic than that of the laughing philosopher, but he
too has a poor opinion of the intellectual achievements of man. The
laughter of one did not stem the tide of tears in the other, and
Saavedra himself was amused "to see that Democritus laughed
because the other would not smile, and Heraclitus grieved because
the other would not weep" (p. 170).

Having reached the brink of negation in his journey through the
Republic of Letters, Saavedra, in the closing pages of his critique,
retreats from his condemnation of the arts and sciences. After his
encounter with Democritus and Heraclitus he reflects:

. . . I could not but think that both the one and the other inveighed too
maliciously against the sciences, which are a sort of attribute annexed to the

Divine Being. For what is poetry but a divine spark, lighted up in but a few? And what is rhetoric but an inspiration from above to influence us to virtue? History but the looking glass of Jove that shows time past, present, and future? Or natural philosophy but the energy of His power, as moral philosophy is but the richness of His goodness or astronomy is a sample of His greatness? And arithmetic, what is it but His discourse bounded only by His essence and majesty? Geometry but the instrument He made all things by, in weight, number, and measure? And law but the execution of His justice? Or physics but a demonstration of His loving kindness? (pp. 170 - 71).

Saavedra's last adventure in the Republic occurred when he saw the Italian physician and scholar, Julius Caesar Scaliger, gagged and manacled, being dragged off to be tried. He was followed by Ovid, Plautus, Terence, Propertius, Tibullus, Claudian, Statius, Silius Italicus, Lucan, Horace, Juvenal, Persius, and Martial. They were all maimed and bore scars. One was without a nose, another without an eye. Some had false teeth and hair, others wooden arms and legs. Ovid makes the accusation. Scaliger is responsible for their maimed bodies and mangled countenances, he says. In the midst of his peroration, the judges are called away by another commotion, and the poets fall upon the hapless Scaliger. Out of compassion for the scholar, Saavedra tries to appease the poets, but he comes to blows with Claudian. Raising his fist in a passion, he strikes it against the bedstead in which he is sleeping and ends his dream.

I awoke [he concludes his book] out of the multitude of errors which I had been in while asleep, perceiving the vanity of our fatigue, wakefulness, and laborious studies, and that it is not he that is farthest advanced in the arts and sciences who is wise, but he who has true and just notions of things; who, regardless of the vulgar herd's light and vain beliefs, lets pass for true only those opinions which really are so . . . . (p. 186).

IV   *The Theme*

Many details in *Republic of Letters* remind us of the old university city of Salamanca and of the University itself. But if Salamanca and its "republic of letters" are the microcosmos, the world of European letters and learning is the cosmos. Saavedra begins his book with these words: "I was running over in my mind the prodigious number and continual increase of books, through the liberty of the press and the presumption of writers who make a downright trade of it, when, falling asleep, a veil was drawn over those images which my thoughts, while awake, had been employed about" (pp. 1 - 2).

Saavedra was writing only a century and a half after the introduction of movable type; and book publishing, especially from the end of the sixteenth century on, was an ever-expanding activity. In *Republic of Letters* he questions whether the vulgarization of learning—especially of that learning which may be deemed false or falsified—is desirable. His answer is equivocal.

He himself confessed his "license and boldness" in the dedication which he wrote to the Count-Duke of San Lúcar (that is, Olivares). His seventeenth-century readers also recognized the dangerous ground on which he trod. "It cannot be denied that the subject matter is both strange and disagreeable, for an esteemed and noble pen is reprehending learning." Thus wrote the canon Francisco Ignacio de Porres in the first printed edition that bore Saavedra's name.[14]

A modern critic, Vicente García de Diego, exonerates Saavedra of the charge of formal skepticism. The young man was heir to the mystic literature of the sixteenth century which was filled with that disdain for earthly things and secular knowledge which the mystic professed in his reach for a luminous union with the eternal. Furthermore, Saavedra became a man in the first years of a century whose theme was to be disillusion—*desengaño* in Spanish. The attitude fed on a spiritual state common to mankind in hours or days of despair and impotence. "We carry in ourselves," García de Diego comments, "the perennial contradiction between our infinite anxiety for the truth and the poverty of our means of attaining it. . . ."[15]

Recently another critic, Ruth Lundelius, has taken an opposing view, and her arguments tend to support an opinion that Menéndez y Pelayo expressed earlier. She demonstrates that Saavedra owes much to Cicero's *Academics* and something to Diogenes Laertius and Sextus Empiricus. The Academic skeptics of which Cicero writes held that certain knowledge of anything was impossible. Lundelius reminds us that Cicero dedicated his *Academics* to Marcus Terentius Varro, who was Saavedra's principal guide. Furthermore, two figures in *Republic of Letters* that give expression to skeptical ideas are Heraclitus and Democritus, who were esteemed as precursors by the skeptic schools. In concluding that Saavedra, like Cicero, viewed learning from the point of view of the man of practical affairs, she explains the contradictions in his ideas that caused García de Diego and Menéndez y Pelayo to take opposing views.[16]

In support of Lundelius's position, it can be pointed out that

Saavedra's readers of the seventeenth century relished his skepticism. Ignacio de Porres, in the prologue to the 1670 edition of *Republic of Letters*, praises him by calling him "the Carneades of our century."[17] The subtle dialectician Carneades, as Cicero tells us, once scandalized Romans by giving, on succeeding days, equally persuasive lectures for and against justice. While Saavedra did not shock his contemporaries, he did, as Lundelius shows, give balanced arguments for and against various issues.

Saavedra Fajardo was both a practical man and a man of action. The sciences—the word should be taken to mean all branches of human knowledge—were, in his view, theoretical and speculative; and the men who cultivated them were, to his mind, inept in practical affairs. A meeting of ancient philosophers and historians results in nonsensical decisions that produce laughter in prudent men. He caricatures men of science. He disdains the scholar, the humanist, who studies ancient medals and stones, who visits ruins, or who laboriously reads old manuscripts. In political science, he despises theory and exalts experience. In the life of the republic he esteems work over study. However, Saavedra was a cultivated man as well as a practical one. When he realizes the abyss which he has approached, he hesitates, pauses to reflect, and then recognizes the value of theoretical knowledge. "Learned men defend their cities no less than soldiers," he confesses. "Only excess can be dangerous."[18]

Republic of Letters is, then, what Saavedra confessed it to be, a "felony" that he committed in his youth. With age he corrected certain irreverent ideas which he had expounded. Yet he preserved throughout his life the fundamental attitude of doubt toward theoretical as opposed to practical wisdom.

Saavedra's posture about the publishing of books is woven into seventeenth-century Spanish attitudes. His work seems to crystallize a position toward which Spanish society was moving. A central episode of the little treatise takes place in the customhouse where censors review books from all over the world. "These loads of books were put under the examination of several grave censors, each reviewing those books that fell under his profession. After a strict perusal, they only admitted for the service of the republic such as were the genuine issue of their authors and well done, such as might improve the understanding and be of use to mankind" (pp. 37 - 38).

Saavedra treats the censors sympathetically. They are worthy men of judgment, capable of deciding what ought to be read and what ought to be used as scrap paper for menial purposes. They demonstrate a sense of humor in the disposition of the paper on which the books are printed, but they are grave and adamant in their execution of their decision. They remind us that every book in seventeenth-century Spain had to have the approval of both civil and ecclesiastical authorities. When *Republic of Letters* itself was finally printed in 1655, it had passed the scrutiny of three censors. The first "approbation" was given in Madrid on April 10 by the Licentiate Don Agustín de Carvajal, who found in it "no doctrine opposed to the Catholic religion which we profess, nor to decent manners which we ought to observe. . . . "[19] The next day, Juan Álvarez de Llamas, in the name of Dr. Juan de Narbona, Vicar of Madrid and a consultant of the Holy Office of the Inquisition, granted the Ordinary's (that is, the Bishop's) license. Finally, at the request of royal authorities, the Benedictine friar Diego Niseno reviewed the work, found nothing contradictory to the Catholic faith nor damaging to the decorum of Christian manners, and recommended approval on May 31.

Cervantes, in *Don Quixote,* presents to us a curious view of censorship. Heir to the Renaissance, writing at the beginning of the century while Saavedra Fajardo was still a university youth, he treats censorship with that irony that is typical of the Cervantine point of view. In Chapter VI of Part I, the censors are the village priest, the local barber, Don Quixote's niece, and his housekeeper. While the knight is asleep after returning from his first sally, the curate asks for the key to the room where the hidalgo keeps the books that were responsible for his troubles. Both women favor throwing the whole lot—more than a hundred large-sized volumes and a number of smaller ones—into a bonfire in the courtyard. However, the curate insists that the books must be scrutinized, and he and the barber pardon a fair number from the fate to which they consign most of the knight's library.

The burning of the books in *Don Quixote* has been interpreted by many critics, and by the creators of modern cinema versions, as an attack on censorship. The seventeenth-century Spanish reader must have had quite a different point of view. He must have thought, "Good riddance to bad rubbish." The niece and the housekeeper were extremists, to be sure; but the curate and the barber were performing a useful service, not unlike that which the censors of Saavedra's customhouse rendered.

A similar "useful" service was performed by the Spanish Inquisition. Its foundation coincided with the introduction of printing into Spain, but in its early years it was more preoccupied with heresies,

especially the backsliding of converted Jews and Muslims. But with
the spread of Protestantism in Europe—into the very domains of
His Most Catholic Majesty—the printed book became a purveyor of
both heresy and treason. The first Spanish Index of prohibited
books appeared in 1551. Four more were published in the sixteenth
century. As the seventeenth century wore on, as flesh-and-blood
heretics were unmasked and eliminated, the Inquisition turned
more and more to the heresies to be found in printed books until
censorship became one of its principal activities. The irony of Cervantes and the satire of Saavedra Fajardo could be turned into support of the practice of censorship. Books that are inept, books that
are offensive to public decorum, books that undermine the
faith—all can be assigned to oblivion. This·is the route that censorship took in Spain as literary judgments became confused with
the aims of the Counter-Reformation.

A different story was being enacted in England in the same
period. Like Henry VIII's break with Rome, it was sparked by a
case for divorce. When, after a month of marriage, John Milton's
wife fled his household to return home, the poet determined to
divorce her. To justify this proposed course of action—which he did
not take, by the way—he published two pamphlets in 1643 and
1644, and raised a storm of controversy. Furthermore, he incurred
the displeasure of the Stationers' Company, which had just been
granted new authority for registering and licensing all publications.
Milton had not obtained permission for the divorce pamphlets, and
the Stationers' Company brought a complaint before the House of
Commons.

Milton counterattacked in the most eloquent of all his prose
writings, *Areopagitica, a Speech of Mr. John Milton for the Liberty
of Unlicenc'd Printing, to the Parlament of England*. It appeared in
November, 1644. Saavedra Fajardo was in Münster at the time,
engaged in the discussions that were later to bring an end to the
Thirty Years' War with the Peace of Westphalia. Milton's pamphlet
was a remonstrance which attacked the whole system of licensing
and censorship of the press, and called for the repeal of the licensing ordinance of 1643. He did not at once succeed in his immediate
aim, but he dealt a death blow to a system which never was able to
marshall its forces against the ideas that Milton so forcefully expressed in this popular pamphlet. "Though all the winds of doctrine
were let loose to play upon the earth," wrote Milton, "so Truth be
in the field, we do unjuriously, by licensing and prohibiting, to mis-
doubt her strength. Let her and Falsehood grapple: who ever knew
Truth put to the worse in a free and open encounter?"[20]

In these words we see a clear division between the Spanish world, where the authoritarian intellect determines what shall be read, and the Anglo-Saxon, where the ideal, at least, is that free minds will winnow and sift to find the grains of truth amidst the chaff of lies. Saavedra Fajardo's *Republic of Letters* is a worthy expression of a point of view, acceptable or not, that had validity in its time and still commands adherents today.

V   *The Sources*

Saavedra Fajardo's sources for *Republic of Letters* are to be found in the whole range of knowledge of his time. In this thin volume he cites 265 names, many of them writers. They range from Anaxarchus, the fourth-century Greek skeptic philosopher, to Jerónimo de Zurita, the sixteenth-century Aragonese historian; from Greek Homer to the greatest poet of his own day, Luis de Góngora. The weight of authority counted for much in Saavedra's time, and the young man brought to bear everything he had learned at the university.

Nevertheless, the presence of two works is especially notable in *Republic of Letters*. García de Diego detected the influence of a brief Latin tract, *Veritas Fucata, sive de Licentia Poetica, Quantum Poetis Liceat a Veritate Abscedere* (*Truth Bedaubed, or On Poetic License: How Far May Poets Depart from the Truth?*).[21] It was written by the Valencian humanist Juan Luis Vives (1492 - 1540), who dated it at Louvain, in Flemish Brabant, on April 1, 1519. There Vives had become friendly with Desiderius Erasmus (1466? - 1536). Thus *Truth Bedaubed* in turn owes a debt to Erasmus's *Encomium Moriae* (*Praise of Folly*, 1509), which had appeared a decade earlier.

Truth Bedaubed and *Republic of Letters* do not have the same critical orientation. Vives composed his tract as a preamble to his inspirational *Triunfo de Cristo* (*Triumph of Christ*). Truth is placed in opposition to Falsehood, and Poetry is likened to the embellishments with which painted women bedaub themselves—hence the title of the tract. The creations of poets, Vives says, citing St. Jerome, are the food of the devils. To him, Homer is a mad old man who relished Falsehood and created a vagrant loafer in the character of Ulysses. The short treatise ends with Truth's appeal to mortal man to embrace her, unembellished though she is; and she promises to lead him in the path of righteousness. The similarity of the two works lies in the light, jocose tone. Furthermore, there is a resemblance in the peripatetic plots, if they can be called that.

However, *Truth Bedaubed* is but a brief sketch, an incident, an allegorical prologue, while *Republic of Letters* is a book, albeit a short one, that has a sequential narrative.

Saavedra's debt to another book, Cornelius Heinrich Agrippa's *Vanity of the Arts and Sciences* (1530), has been conclusively demonstrated by Ruth Lundelius.[22] She believes and convincingly argues that Saavedra Fajardo must have had Agrippa's book before him as he composed *Republic of Letters*. Agrippa (1486 - 1535), a native of Cologne, Germany, was a physician, a theologian, and a student of the occult. He was both an adventurer and a scholar, a Doctor of Divinity, a Doctor of Medicine, and a Doctor of Law. To the Roman Church of his day he was a controversial figure.

When he composed *Vanity of the Arts and Sciences*, in 1526, he was supposedly employed as a physician to Louise of Savoy, Queen Mother of Francis I of France; and he was living at her court in Lyons. He had turned down several dazzling offers in order to accept the post, and then Louise did not pay his salary. The opposition to his ideas by priests and courtiers served as a pretext for the avaricious queen to go back on her word. Agrippa suffered real hardships, and his disillusionment over the worth of his learning is reflected in his book. "Nihil scire felicissima vita"—("To know nothing is the happiest life") was the motto he placed on the title page. In 102 chapters Agrippa reviews the sciences, the arts, and the nature of man; and he inveighs against almost every branch of knowledge. Thus he sought to even the score with those supposedly learned men who had undermined him in the queen's favor. The book is heavy with erudition. His pedantry contrasts with the light touch of Saavedra in *Republic of Letters*.

Yet, as Ruth Lundelius proves by juxtaposing passages from the two books, Saavedra's debt to Agrippa is a direct one. Saavedra condenses and rearranges material; he omits data, adds new bits of information, and reshuffles elements. He divides a passage from Agrippa and uses one part in one place and the rest in another; or he may select scattered items from his source and combine them in one place. Lundelius cites at least twenty sets of parallel passages which support her contention that Saavedra did not rely on memory alone but must have had Agrippa's book at hand. Furthermore, she observes: "Passages which do not correspond closely nevertheless betray an undeniable influence, and in all the subjects discussed by Saavedra Fajardo none of his opinions contradicts those of Agrippa."[23]

Both Agrippa and Saavedra are name-droppers, and in the

evidence of proper names Lundelius finds further proof of Saavedra's debt to *Vanity of the Arts and Sciences.* Saavedra mentions some 265 proper names in *Republic of Letters.* Of these, 144—more than half—are found in *Vanity.* Besides, both authors often make the same observations about the same figure in phraseology that is similar. For example, both speak of the common scorn for poetry shared by Cato and Aulus Gellius; both mention Plato's dislike for rhetoricians and Licinius's scorn for learning. To be sure, Agrippa uses four times as many names as Saavedra. He liked to show off his erudition, while Saavedra demonstrates concern for his reader by selecting only the more significant names. The Spaniard mentions 121 names that are not found in Agrippa. They are mostly men who lived after Agrippa, many contemporaries of Saavedra. Spanish and Italian names are most frequent. They do not, however, introduce new topics but instead enlarge upon a subject already found in Agrippa.

Some of the names that Saavedra included in a manuscript of *Republic of Letters* are omitted in the first printed edition. One of these is the name of Agrippa himself along with the entire passage in which he is cited as a magician. The censors, or perhaps self-censorship, may have been at work, for, as Lundelius points out, the names of all Jews are also omitted from *Republic of Letters.*[24]

A common source for much of the facile erudition evident in the name-dropping was available to both Agrippa and Saavedra in Polydore Vergil's *The Inventors of Things.* Vergil was Agrippa's contemporary, but his book first appeared in 1499 so that it was widely available by the time Agrippa was writing. Saavedra Fajardo, when he was doing *Republic of Letters,* had available to him Juan de la Cueva's Spanish translation of 1607. Thus, the author Polydore Vergil provided either directly, or indirectly through Agrippa, a lot of superficial erudition and also became a character—one of the guides—in *Republic of Letters.*

VI *Bibliographical History*

The manuscripts and printed texts of *Republic of Letters* have presented a series of problems which are interesting to people who enjoy puzzles. In a series of three articles I have unravelled some of the mysteries.[25] Here I shall give a summary of the peripatetic history of the manuscripts and editions of the little masterpiece. In 1612 Saavedra wrote a primitive version of some 12,500 words, which I call the "short" text. It circulated in manuscript, and has survived in a single manuscript, number 7526, which is in the National Library in Madrid.

A manuscript copy of the short text came into the possession of Antonio de Arana (1588 - 1650), who was almost an exact contemporary of Saavedra himself. He was a Jesuit, and after his death his papers, in six folio volumes, entered the library of the Jesuit Imperial College in Madrid. More than a century later, in 1767, the Jesuits were expelled from Spain, and the College became the secularized Royal School of St. Isidore. There were, to be sure, priests as well as laymen on the faculty and staff, and among the priests was a librarian named Pedro Estala (1759? - 1815), a close friend of Juan Pablo Forner and Leandro Fernández de Moratín. Estala discovered the manuscript among Arana's papers, recognized its resemblance to *República literaria*, and published it, in 1792 or 1793, in an irregular serial periodical called *Gabinete de Lectura Española* (*Spanish Reading Room*). It bore the long title *Discurso curioso, agudo y erudito acerca de la multitud de libros que cada día se publican, y juicio de los autores en todas facultades así modernos como antiguos* (*Curious, Keen, and Erudite Discourse on the Multitude of Books that Are Published Every Day, and Criticism of Authors both Ancient and Modern in Every Discipline*).

While we have Estala's printed text, the fate of the Arana manuscript itself is in doubt. During the Constitutional Triennium of 1820 - 23, the Cortes (Parliament) librarian Bartolomé José Gallardo was assigned to inspect the holdings of the Royal School library and was authorized to transfer to the library of the Cortes the works he considered useful. He took some books and all the manuscripts. When the French invaded Spain in 1823, Gallardo retreated with the Cortes to Seville, carrying with him books and manuscripts from the library. Then the liberals fell back on Cádiz, and Gallardo was fleeing from Seville on June 13 with nine bundles of library materials. He lost them when the populace of the city attacked those liberals who had not yet escaped.

Whether the Arana manuscript underwent and survived these vicissitudes, or whether it simply remained behind in Madrid, I cannot say for certain. The copy in National Library MS. 7526 has pagination that shows that it was formerly part of a different volume, perhaps one of Arana's six folios. It is now in a miscellany that belonged to Juan Vélez de León (1655 - 1736), a man born after Saavedra's death; and the binding of the volume itself was done in the late nineteenth or early twentieth century. The title page is missing, but the text is so close to the one that Estala printed in 1792 - 93—only matters like punctuation and capitalization differ markedly—that I would guess that it is the same manuscript that Arana owned. In 1907 M. Serrano y Sanz published a transcription in an edition of fifty copies. García de Diego in the Clásicos Castellanos edition of *Republic of Letters* and González Palencia in Saavedra's *Obras completas (Complete Works)* of 1946 reprinted it in footnotes. However, this short text has not been accepted as a literary entity in its own right.

Referring to the work he wrote in his youth, Saavedra says that he let the narrative circulate anonymously in Spain and that it was so changed by copyists that he had to rewrite it. He does not say exactly when he revised it, except that he did so before he published *Idea de un príncipe político-cristiano (The Royal Politician)* in 1640. Sometime between 1640 and January of 1643, he wrote a dedication to the Count-Duke of San Lúcar (Olivares), whose fall from favor occurred in the latter year, but Saavedra still did not print his narrative. A rough draft *(borrador)* of this revised manuscript survives in the National Library as MS. 6436. It is in a hand unknown to me, probably that of a professional amanuensis; but it has corrections and additions in Saavedra's own handwriting. This is the "long" version; it has some twenty-five thousand words, or double the number of the short text.

It appears that at least two copies were made from this rough draft. One of them came into the possession of either Don Melchor de Fonesca y Almeida or Don Gaspar de Seixas Vasconcelos, who collaborated in printing it. Either these two or someone before them conspired to conceal Saavedra's authorship, for they omitted the introductory material and one passage in the text identifying Saavedra as the author. Neither claims the work as his own, however. They attribute it to Don Claudio Antonio de Cabrera. Since there is no other evidence for the existence of such a person, we can presume that Fonesca and Seixas created for Saavedra the penname of Cabrera. They used the title *Juizio de artes y sciencias (Criticism of Arts and Sciences)*. The book was published seven years after Saavedra's death (Madrid: Julián de Paredes, 1655). Thus, the first printed edition of Saavedra's little masterpiece bore neither his name nor the title that he gave it in the rough draft. Doubtless for these reasons this edition did not give rise to subsequent ones, although its existence has been well known.

We have documentation concerning the other copy that must have been made from the rough draft. It was in the library of Don Antonio de Aragón. This young nobleman and churchman was related to Cardinal Gaspar de Borja, Saavedra's chief. Borja was in Madrid in the 1640's until his death in 1645, and Aragón and Saavedra were there off and on between 1643 and Saavedra's death in 1648. It is plausible that during that time Aragón came into possession of a manuscript which his secretary called an "original" one. We must, of course, distinguish this "original" smooth copy from the rough draft, which is MS. 6436. The secretary was Don José de Salinas, who also served Don Antonio de Aragón as librarian for his fine collection of books. Aragón had Salinas make a copy of the "original." The secretary must have done this at some time between the 1640's, when Don Antonio obtained the "original," and 1660, when he died.

Don Antonio's younger brother, Don Pascual de Aragón, inherited the library. That same year he was named a cardinal and appointed Spanish ambassador to Rome. He moved bag and baggage, taking his brother's library with him. On the voyage, disaster struck. The galleons that bore Don Pascual and his household suffered shipwreck. Although Don Pascual survived, his library was lost. Among the treasures that disappeared was the "original" manuscript of *Republic of Letters* that Don Antonio had owned.

However, the copy that Don José de Salinas had made must have remained behind in Spain, for he and Dr. Francisco Ignacio de Porres used it for the first printed edition which bore the title *República literaria* and the name of Diego de Saavedra Fajardo (Alcalá de Henares: María Fernández, 1670). It appeared twenty-two years after the author's death. At the time Porres and Salinas were both canons in the magistral church of Saints Justus and Pastor in Alcalá. I have found no trace of the manuscript that they used. The printed text shows few variants from the rough draft (MS. 6436). It is the text from which subsequent printed editions were first derived, and next to MS. 6436 provides the most trustworthy text.

The adventures of Saavedra's text did not end with the printing of it. I shall mention only the more striking vicissitudes that caused modifications in the text. A certain M. F. obtained a copy of the 1670 Alcalá text and published an edition in Brussels in 1677 with the bookdealer Lambert Marchant. In the copy that he used the last page of the text was missing. He completed the broken sentence, but his text is shorter by thirty-one words than the Alcalá edition. The Brussels edition was used in turn by Juan Bautista Verdussen of Antwerp for his 1678 edition. The Verdussen edition was widely distributed in Europe, and as a result the shortened text with the truncated ending was reprinted over and over.

Meanwhile, back in Spain the eighteenth-century scholar Gregorio Mayáns y Siscar much admired Saavedra Fajardo. He wrote a paper about him and also published two editions of *Republic of Letters* (1730, 1735). Mayáns knew both *Criticism of Arts and Sciences* of 1655 and the 1670 Alcalá edition, but he was a devout Roman Catholic and a Neoclassic, and he was a zealot about his beliefs. He thought he could improve on Saavedra's text and set about to do so. He created many variants both of a religious and a literary nature, but I shall mention only one as an example. At the beginning of the book Saavedra describes the entrance to the Republic of Letters where statues of the Muses stand in niches between marble and jasper columns. By name, Saavedra speaks of six of them, but he says nothing of the other three. The omission was more than Mayáns's orderly mind could bear. He included the other three Muses by name and described their roles.

Mayáns's text was very successful, for most subsequent Spanish editions were based on it. Although the editors of the Biblioteca de Autores Españoles (Vol. 25, 1853) were acquainted with the rough draft (MS. 6436) in the National Library, they printed only Saavedra's dedication and prologue from it. For the text itself they used the Mayáns version as it appeared in the 1788 Madrid edition. Not until 1922 was the text of the rough draft printed. Vicente García de Diego transcribed it for the Clásicos Castellanos edition, and, since then, it has become the standard text.

The Mayáns version or the Antwerp or Brussels editions were used by translators. The Flemish texts with the truncated ending served as the basis for two translations into English, one published in London in 1705, and the other in both London and Dublin in 1727 and 1728. We may surmise that Jonathan Swift knew either the 1705 translation or one of the Spanish editions. In *Gulliver's Travels*, Book III, Chapters VII and VIII, the protagonist visits the island of Glubbdubdrib, a land of sorcerers and magicians, The governor of the island has "the power of calling whom he pleaseth from the Dead, and commanding their service for twenty four Hours, but no longer. . . . "[26] Gulliver himself is permitted to call up whatever persons he "would chuse to name, and in whatever Numbers among all the Dead from the Beginning of the World to the present time. . . . " The ensuing "vision," in which he converses with men of former times, recalls so clearly that of Saavedra in *Republic of Letters* that we must wonder whether Swift did not know this book. Among the spirits conjured up by Gulliver is Polydore Vergil, one of Saavedra's fictional guides as well as a main source of his information.

The Mayáns text was used for versions in German (Leipzig, 1748), Italian (Pisa, 1767), and French (Lausanne, 1770). The most curious of these books is the Italian. It is a version, not a translation, done by Francesco Gerbault. The Mayáns text served him merely as a point of departure. Taking his cue from Saavedra himself, who quoted a mere two verses of Michelangelo, Gerbault introduces extensive quotations from Dante, Petrarch, Ariosto, Guarini, Tasso, Gabriello Chiabrera, Marino, Francesco Redi, and even poets of his own day. Gerbault also expands on the text at will so that in his version Saavedra's "little masterpiece" has become inflated and pretentious.

The European vogue of *Republic of Letters* began in 1677 and lasted a hundred years. This period coincided with the flowering of that international intellectual society which men of learning were pleased to call the Republic of Letters, a term especially dear to one of the luminaries of the period, Jean Le Clerc (1657 - 1736).[27] Men of letters produced volumes, usually in Latin but sometimes in the vernacular, that extolled the intellectual accomplishments of their kind, both past and present. The ponderous titles began *Catalogue of Illustrious Writers . . . , Learned France . . . ,* or *History of Female Philosophers. . . .*[28] Saavedra's thin volume does not belong in the same category with these works either in depth or intent. If the title goes back to 1612, however, as MS. 6436 suggests, or even to the 1640's, then it antedates the wide employment of the term as applied to the world of learning, and the book's later popularity may have contributed to the use of the phrase.

Nevertheless, *Republic of Letters* satirized the realm of the arts and sciences and its devotion to the publication of books. Contrary to the weighty tomes that exalted the world of learning, Saavedra's work questions the basic values which sustained that world. One can imagine that learned people read it precisely because they liked his spoof of the cult of learning.

CHAPTER 2

The Art of Propaganda

SAAVEDRA Fajardo penned the prologue "To the Reader" of his *Idea de un príncipe político-cristiano* (*The Royal Politician*) in 1640. There he says that he wrote the book in order that the world might not lose the experience that he had acquired during the thirty-four years, following five years of study at Salamanca, which he had spent "in the principal courts of Europe, engaged always in public affaris."[1]

It is plausible, therefore, to suppose that he went to Rome, the court of the papacy, soon after he received his bachelor's degree at Salamanca, April 21, 1606, as a youth of twenty-two. He may have spent two more years at Salamanca, so that his departure for Rome would have been in 1608 when he was twenty-four, but the record is not clear on this point. It is logical to presume that about this time he took minor orders. A young man who took the "first tonsure," as it was called, made no lasting commitment. He shaved the crown of his head and did not marry as long as he was in orders. He could be considered eligible for certain church benefices, which served the purpose of fellowships and gave him a small income while he was getting started in life. In the eighteenth century he would have been, in France, the *petit abbé*, in Spain, the *abate*, both famous in the life and literature of the day as salon dandies, music and dancing masters, gossips, and busybodies. In Saavedra's time, the men in minor orders seem to have been a more serious lot. There is no evidence, however, that Saavedra ever went beyond the first tonsure to enter the priesthood.

In Rome—at what date we do not know—he became associated with Don Gaspar de Borja y Velasco (1580 - 1645), younger brother of the Duke of Gandía. This Spanish Levant family—Valencia, Játiva, Gandía, and Murcia are among the principal cities of the region—is better known in history under the Italian spelling of their name, Borgia. Don Gaspar, four years older than Saavedra, had

47

gone to Rome, also at the age of twenty-two, in 1602. He was the
sedate descendant of noted and notorious ancestors who had made
their mark on Rome. Rodrigo Borja or Borgia (1431 - 1503) was
born at Játiva near Gandía. A cardinal at age twenty-five, and later
Bishop of Valencia, Porto, and Cartagena, he was elected Pope in
1492 as Alexander VI and two years later apportioned the New
World between Spain and Portugal. He was known as an able ad-
ministrator, a patron of the arts and sciences, and a friend of the
people. He also condemned the rebellious Dominican reformer
Girolamo Savonarola to be burned as a heretic.

His beautiful mistress Vanozza Catanei bore him four sons and a
daughter, among them Giovanni, Duke of Gandía, Cesare Borgia,
and Lucrezia Borgia. Lucrezia was first married at thirteen, again at
eighteen, and finally at twenty-one. Although it was said that she
participated with Cesare in all the crime, vice, and licentiousness of
the time, after her third marriage she settled down as Duchess of
Ferrara, patronized literature, and encouraged the writer Pietro
Bembo.

Cesare Borgia (c. 1476 - 1507) followed in his father's footsteps,
though he did not go so far. He too became a priest, though neither
priesthood nor the papacy nor even sainthood kept the men of this
family from fathering a numerous progeny. Cesare became
archbishop of Valencia, and in 1493, shortly after his father became
Pope, he was made a cardinal, at the age of seventeen if his supposed date of birth is correct. Later he abandoned the priesthood
and resigned the cardinalate. His importance to the Church lay in
his unification of the Papal States, and such was both his astuteness
and his military prowess that he has been considered the model for
Machiavelli's *The Prince* (1513). Cesare Borgia belonged to the age
of the explorers and the conquistadores. His collateral descendant
Don Gaspar and the latter's secretary Saavedra Fajardo belonged to
the period of consolidation and conservation, and Saavedra's
greatest book *The Royal Politician* was devoted to combating the
prevalent Machiavellian philosophy which the actions of Cesare
Borgia had inspired and which Machiavelli had codified.

The Borja family produced another contrasting strain of character
in the sixteenth century. Don Francisco de Borja y Aragón (1510 -
1572) was the great-grandson on his father's side of Pope Alexander
VI and on his mother's side of King Ferdinand the Catholic, who
also had some claims to being the model for Machiavelli's *Prince*.
Don Francisco is known to us as St. Francis Borgia, one of the first
and most resolute followers of St. Ignatius of Loyola. He married at

nineteen and had a family. His wife died when he was thirty-six. He then professed in the Company of Jesus and became a priest in 1551 at the age of forty-one. The Saint's son and heir, Don Carlos, was a soldier; and his grandson, Don Francisco de Borja y Aragón (1581 - 1658), a cousin and contemporary of Don Gaspar, distinguished himself as a lyric poet.

The Rome of the first years of the seventeenth century was not the licentious capital of Christendom that it had been under Don Gaspar's ancestor Alexander VI. The spirit of the Counter-Reformation had had its effect. The outward tone of the city was serious, and if puritanism did not run deep, the Papal States nevertheless appeared to have a distinctly higher moral tone than had prevailed in the days of the Renaissance Popes. Rome had become, in fact, the seat of a great bureaucracy, and Don Gaspar de Borja and Saavedra Fajardo were a part of it. The trajectory of the Borja family from Don Rodrigo the Renaissance pope, through Don Francisco the militant saint, to Don Francisco the poet and Don Gaspar the bureaucrat, is like a microcosmos of Catholic Europe from the end of the fifteenth century to the beginning of the seventeenth.

I *In the Service of the Cardinal*

Like several of his ancestors Don Gaspar was proposed for the cardinalate. Paul V made him cardinal on August 17, 1611, when he had attained the age of thirty-one; and on November 27, 1612, he received the hat from the hands of the Pontiff. Saavedra Fajardo was with him to celebrate the event. His position was that of *letrado de cámara*, which we can explain rather than translate as "personal attorney." He also called himself on occasion Don Gaspar's secretary. In modern terms, we can think of him as administrative assistant to the young cardinal. Saavedra served him in this capacity for the next twenty-two years until 1633. Don Gaspar was interim ambassador for Spain in Rome from 1616 to 1619 and ambassador from 1631 to 1635.[2] During these years in the service of the cardinal, Saavedra held other posts and received special assignments. While Don Gaspar was interim ambassador and for two years afterward, from 1616 to 1621, Saavedra handled the affairs of Naples and Sicily in Rome. Both times that the Cardinal was ambassador Saavedra served as first secretary, handling all papers and ciphers.

Saavedra also sought to augment his income with the fruits of church benefices. The first attempt of which we have a record was not successful. Juan Genesio, agent in Rome for the cathedral chapter of Murcia, died in 1613. Saavedra Fajardo solicited the post of representative of the cathedral in his native province, but he was rejected.[3] The next year the doctoral canonship of the Murcia cathedral fell vacant. If the chapter did not fill the post within six months, then the Pope had the right to do so. The chapter, trying to get new statutes approved before the replacement was named, let the time slip by. Apparently Saavedra and Cardinal Borja enjoyed the good will of Paul V, because the Pope named Saavedra to the post as soon as the six months had passed. In letters to the chapter, its agents in Rome stated that Saavedra was an excellent person, very studious, and capable of filling the post with dignity. He was, they wrote, discreet and prudent, and he did not want to engage in disputes. By accepting the post, he kept it from falling into the hands of someone perhaps unacceptable to the chapter. Obviously, both Saavedra and the agents hoped that the chapter would be agreeable to his continuing in the job. However, the chapter chose in the end to nominate someone else, and Saavedra gracefully withdrew.[4]

He was more successful in 1617 when he was awarded a canonry in the Metropolitan Church of Santiago de Compostela, on the opposite side of the peninsula from Murcia. A dispensation from the Pope permitted him to collect the emoluments without actually residing in Compostela. When the cathedral chapter objected to this convenient arrangement, Saavedra presented additional letters from Rome and offered to serve as agent to handle the cathedral's affairs in the Eternal City. The chapter was in need of help because the position of Santiago (St. James) as patron saint of Spain was being undermined by Carmelite propaganda in favor of St. Teresa. Saavedra won from the Congregation of Rites in Rome a privilege for the prayer of the Apostle St. James to be said every Monday in the cathedral. In return for his services, he expected prompt payment of the income from his benefice.[5] He held another benefice in the church of Fuente Rapel in the archdiocese of León, and during a trip to Madrid in 1622 he gave a power of attorney for the collection of the money owed him.[6]

Some years later Saavedra succeeded in obtaining a benefice in the cathedral at Cartagena, which is on the coast a short distance from Murcia. In 1627 Pope Urban VIII granted a vacant precentorship there. Saavedra wrote cordially to the chapter regretting that he could not personally come to take possession of the post but offering in recompense to look after the chapter's business in Rome.

The chapter permitted a proxy to take office for him, and then Saavedra and Borja wrote begging the chapter to consider the new cantor as if present, since he had to reside in Rome as agent for His Majesty the King. The chapter was reluctant to allow this continued nonresidence, and Saavedra had to get two papal briefs in order to prolong his absence and at the same time collect his money. Also, he still held only minor orders; that is, he had never been ordained in the priesthood. Another papal brief was required to silence the objections of the chapter on this point. The situation went on for more than three years. Realizing that the chapter was not going to continue its benevolence, Saavedra succeded in getting the Pope to transfer the precentorship to his nephew Juan de Saavedra.[7]

Saavedra's reluctance to isolate himself in provincial Spanish cities is understandable, for life in Italy was far more stimulating than it could possibly be in Cartagena, Murcia, or Santiago de Compostela. In 1620 an adventure in the Kingdom of Naples provided Cardinal Borja and his secretary Saavedra with an exciting interlude away from their routine in Rome. Philip III had determined to get rid of the Duke of Osuna as Viceroy of Naples, and he appointed Cardinal Borja as interim Viceroy, a post which seems to have brought to the surface the latent Borja arrogance. The Neapolitans, displeased with the government of Osuna (whom the writer Francisco de Quevedo served as secretary), were glad to learn that he would be replaced, and they urged Cardinal Borja to hasten his arrival. Accompanied by Saavedra, Borja traveled from Rome to the fortified seaport of Gaeta north of the Bay of Naples. From there he informed Osuna of his arrival but received no reply. He then sent his secretary to interview Osuna. Saavedra missed seeing Quevedo, for the Duke had sent him back to Spain with messages for the King, but he carried out his mission with Osuna. By June 3 Borja had taken possession of the office of Viceroy, and on June 20 Osuna set sail for Spain. During the ensuing months Saavedra served Viceroy Borja as Secretary of State and War.[8]

The Neapolitans were not happy with their new governor, either. One historian has commented that they "gained little with the departure of the Duke of Osuna, whom they accused of arrogant conduct, for they fell into the hands of the Cardinal. He reimposed the taxes that his predecessor had revoked, and he rivaled him in haughtiness though he did not possess his talents."[9] At the end of the year Borja was replaced by another Spanish cardinal, Antonio Zapata. Borja left Naples for Rome on December 14, and presumably Saavedra Fajardo accompanied him. On his return from

Naples, Cardinal Borja attended the conclave for the election of a
new Pope, and Saavedra was present in his capacity as secretary.
Elected to succeed to the papacy on February 9, 1621, was the
Bolognese Cardinal Alessandro Ludovici who became Gregory XV.

Saavedra made a trip to Spain in 1622. A new monarch sat on the
Spanish throne. The pious Philip III, who took little interest in
government, had gone to meet his Maker the year before, and his
seventeen-year-old son succeeded him as Philip IV. The new reign
had not yet defined itself, but already Don Gaspar de Guzmán, later
Count-Duke of Olivares, controlled the government as favorite and
prime minister of the young king. The painter Diego de Silva
Velázquez still lived in Sevilla. The following year he would come
to Madrid as painter to the king to begin recording both the
beautiful and the grotesque aspects of a brilliant society in decline.

Those were perilous times as Hapsburg Spain fought the tides of
Protestantism and the increasing power of Bourbon France in a
struggle that was to be known as the Thirty Years' War (1618 -
1648). Six years after the beginning of his reign Philip IV sum-
marized, in a message to his parliament, the state of the monarchy,
as he had found it on the death of his father:

I found the treasury so exhausted that all its resources were anticipated
for years to come. . . . The currency of my kingdoms had been inflated to
three times its real value. . . . Ecclesiastical affairs were in such disorder
that it was asserted from Rome that a large number of dispensations for
simony had been obtained for bishoprics and archbishoprics, not to mention an even larger number for prebends. . . .

The judiciary was in such a state that on the first day of my reign I had to
take those decisive steps that are familiar to you. The executive branch I
found in much the same situation. I put it briefly when I say that the
ministers who received bribes were more than those who did not.

The monarchy was so discredited that in the truce which the Dutch made
with my father they were treated as independent princes. . . .

I found only seven warships in the fleet. . . . India was lost, and we
were on the point of losing the Indies. . . . Three months after my reign
began, the twelve-year truce with Flanders expired; during it we lost both
control of the country and our reputation. German affairs were so pressing
that it seemed a miracle would be required if we did not lose everything
there.

The marriage of the Prince of Wales, today King of England, to my sister
the Infanta Doña María, now Queen of Hungary, was so far advanced that
it seemed impossible to avoid it without a great war, since we could not
give in on the religious issue.

Portugal was discontent with the government of the Viceroy. The rest of the monarchy was neglected or misgoverned. . . . The kingdom of Naples was near revolt, and the currency was completely debased. . . .[10]

Saavedra, having witnessed the condition of the Spanish empire at the seat of the monarchy, returned to Rome for a second conclave at which Urban VIII was elected Pope on August 6, 1623. Urban's papacy lasted longer than had his predecessor's, for he lived until 1644. In this period members of the Spanish delegation in Rome were obliged to exert to the utmost their diplomatic skills, for Urban sided with the French in the wars. Still, Urban supported Saavedra, recommending him to the Spanish king for a new post, that of Procurator and Solicitor at the Roman court for the kingdom of Castile, the Indies, and the Council of Castile. In this capacity Saavedra rendered services in Rome for which he was paid through his agent in Madrid, Dr. Alonso de Moncada. For example, in 1624 he aided the Sevillian poet and royal chronicler Francisco de Rioja and the Valencian dramatist Guillén de Castro, and in 1626 he helped the Mexican playwright (once his fellow student at Salamanca) Juan Ruiz de Alarcón.[11]

One time his honesty in the handling of such affairs was brought into question. A client complained that Saavedra misused letters of exchange and that his fees were excessive. The king asked the Spanish ambassador to investigate. It seems that the charges may have had some foundation; nevertheless, it was reported that Saavedra was acting within the bounds of current practice in the Holy See. He continued in his post as Solicitor and Procurator until his king chose to call upon him, in 1633, for services of a higher order.

II   *Verse*

The quarter of a century and more that Saavedra spent in Rome was not especially productive in literary works although he was accumulating that fund of experience as a practical man of affairs on which he was later to draw. Aside from *Republic of Letters*, which took its inspiration from his student days, he wrote occasional verse and his first political tracts.

The earliest record we have of Saavedra Fajardo's appearance in print is two poems which formed a part of the introductory matter to a book entitled *Desengaño de Fortuna (Fortune Unmasked)* by Gutierre Marqués de Careaga.[12] It was published in Barcelona in 1611 and in Madrid the next year, 1612, the date that has been assigned to the composition of *Republic of Letters*. There were

twenty contributors of laudatory poems, among them Saavedra and
Juan Ruiz de Alarcón. The versifiers came from all over Spain, from
the Canary Islands, and from Mexico, so that one wonders whether
they had not perhaps been classmates at Salamanca. Marqués de
Careaga was a native of Almería in the one-time kingdom of
Granada; at the time he published the book he was a lieutenant of
the mayor of Madrid.[13] He dedicated the book to Don Rodrigo
Calderón, the jovial and powerful favorite of the dour and pious
Philip III. If Don Rodrigo did not read the book *Fortune Unmasked*, he should have, for when Don Gaspar de Guzmán took
over on the succession of Philip IV to the throne, the future Count-
Duke of Olivares had Don Rodrigo executed on the gallows in the
Plaza Mayor of Madrid. The rise and fall of Rodrigo Calderón
evoked a spate of Baroque reflections on the subject of man's fate
and God's will. In the book of 1611 Saavedra dedicated a Latin
poem to Rodrigo Calderón, and for the author of the book, he, like
Ruiz de Alarcón, composed a single *décima*, a ten-line stanza in
rhymed octosyllabic verses.

More significant than Saavedra's poems is the subject matter of
Marqués de Careaga's book, for the author treats a theme that was
to preoccupy Saavedra himself in *The Royal Politician*: the respec-
tive roles of Fortune and Divine Providence in the affairs of men. In
twenty-three chapters Marqués defines Fortune and distinguishes it
from happenstance, chance, luck, and fate. He emphatically supports Divine Providence as the motivating force in the world.
("There's a special providence in the fall of a sparrow," Shakespeare wrote in *Hamlet*.) He explains why God visits suffering on
men and maintains that no man is called upon to bear more than he
can stand. He insists that the opinion is false which says that Fortune favors those who do not deserve it, and he concludes his
treatise by proving that in fact Fortune does not exist.

Saavedra contributed a Latin poem to the introductory material
of the book which his old teacher Francisco Cascales published in
1614, *Tablas poéticas* (*Principles of Poetics*). Cascales supported
Aristotelian precepts at a time when writers like Lope de Vega were
renouncing them. In his epigram Saavedra admonishes the reader
who would write verse to learn from Cascales's precepts how to
adapt his style to the characters and situations of which he sings.

In 1611, the same year that Marqués de Careaga published *Fortune Unmasked*, the Queen of Spain died. In honor of Margaret of
Austria, wife of Philip III and mother of the six-year-old boy who
would reign as Philip IV, Spanish cities outdid themselves in

observing funeral rites. Spaniards in Rome also mourned the event, and they adorned the church where the ceremony took place with poems written or printed on posters which were hung throughout the temple. These posters illustrated with emblems were well lighted so that mourners of like persuasion might read the verses and reflect on the qualities of the deceased and the fate which awaits all mortals. The poems were collected into a book of fifty-six leaves published that same year.[14] Saavedra's contribution was abundant—a dozen pieces in both Latin and Spanish—as befitted a well-educated Salamanca graduate and rising young diplomat assigned to the Holy See. Neither these poems nor the few remaining examples of his efforts in verse have won him a place among poets in the Spanish Parnassus.

The esteemed sonnet "A una fuente" ("To a Mountain Spring"), which Saavedra included in *Republic of Letters*, may not have been his own, for it has been attributed to at least three other writers. An author would be proud to claim it as his own. It begins with charming metaphors referring to the mountain spring: "Risa del monte, de las aves lira" ("Laughter in the woods, for the birds a lyre"). The reader of Baroque taste savors the hyperbaton and the assonant rhyme of the first and last words, which form the basic metaphors: *risa* and *lira*. Gracián, who printed the poem as an example of an unusual conceit, called it "most perfect," for he found especially attractive the contrast that the poem makes between the clear spring and the turbid human heart.

But does it belong to Saavedra? It is not to be found in the short version of *Republic of Letters*, which circulated in manuscript after 1612. It is included in the long version beginning with MS. 6436, in *Juicio de artes y ciencias* (*Criticism of Arts and Sciences*; 1656), and in the first (1670) and subsequent printed editions entitled *República literaria*. Saavedra pictures the Greek cynic Diogenes isolated from his fellow philosophers. From the bank of a brook he contemplates the current, and in the bark of a poplar tree he carves the words of "this Spanish epigram," that is, the sonnet that begins "Laughter in the woods. . . ."[15] Saavedra does not use the title "To a Mountain Spring." He does not say that the poem is his; neither does he say that it is not.

The poem appeared in print, however, after Saavedra composed his primitive verison of *Republic of Letters* (1612), but before he reworked MS. 6436 (before 1640). Tirso de Molina printed it in *Cigarrales de Toledo* (*Gardens of Toledo*), which may have originally appeared in 1621 although the first extant edition is dated 1624.

In the fourth chapter the characters repair to Isabela's country estate near Toledo. The weather is hot, and Isabela decrees that her guests will amuse themselves in the morning by reciting whatever each person can recall. Narcisa says the poem "To a Mountain Spring," which is given that title in the text. There are major and minor variants between this version and the one in MS. 6436 of *República literaria*. Tirso does not give the name of the author, but he says the poem is by "a prince of Castile, whose genius is equal to his [noble] blood, which is the best in Europe."[16] The guests, applauding Narcisa's recitation, want to know the author, and she promises to tell them "when she has permission to do so." However, the matter does not come up again in the book.

Gracián cited the poem in *Agudeza y arte de ingenio* (*Quickness and Art of Wit*) in 1642, and it is clear that he took it from Tirso's book. His version has only a slight variant from Tirso's, and he too ascribes it to "a prince in blood and more of a prince in genius."[17] Subsequently, the poem has also been ascribed to the Count of Villamediana and to Francisco de Borja y Aragón, Prince of Esquilache (1581 - 1658), a cousin of Saavedra's chief, Don Gaspar. However, we are best advised to accept, as José María Cossío recommends, the attribution "of uncertain authorship" which Juan Nicolás Böhl von Faber used in his *Floresta de rimas antiguas castellanas* (*Anthology of Old Castilian Verse*; 1821 - 25). Saavedra's claim appears as valid as that of the other proposed authors, but it is far from certain.

In 1631, while he was back in Madrid, Saavedra chanced to have the opportunity to participate in an outburst of poetic effort occasioned by a trivial incident. The Count-Duke of Olivares was ever persistent in his efforts to keep Philip IV amused while he ran affairs of state to suit himself. On October 13, in honor of the second birthday of the Crown Prince Baltasar Carlos, whom we know from Velázquez's paintings when he was a bit older, the count-duke put on a Roman festival, which included a fight among several animals: a lion, a tiger, a bear, a bull, a horse, a whippet, and several smaller creatures. It was held in the Plaza del Parque at the Buen Retiro Palace because of the recent fire in the Plaza Mayor. In attendance were the royal family, prelates, counselors, nobles, and a public composed of Spaniards and foreigners. In the struggle, several animals perished; the bull was triumphant. Men entered the ring in an artificial turtle made of wood which moved on wheels, but they failed to kill the bull. The king sensed the gravity of the situation. Since the bull had entered the ring to die in the presence of the monarch, to grant him his life was to punish him, condemning him to die in some less glorious situation. Philip asked for a harquebus, tossed his cape over his shoulder with a gallant gesture, cocked his hat, aimed and fired. The bull fell dead, his blood reddening the earth.

The king's action produced a sensation, and the poets of Spain celebrated the event. The *Anfiteatro de Felipe el Grande* (*Amphitheater of Philip the Great*), published by José Pellicer y Tovar before the year was out, contains works by eighty-eight poets, some of them women. Lope de Vega, besides contributing, was charged with the censorship of the book. Other great lights who figured in the volume were Francisco de Rioja, Quevedo, Rojas Zorrilla, Ruiz de Alarcón, Vélez de Gevara, Calderón, Montalván, and Mira de Amescua.[18] Saavedra Fajardo was represented with a poem of two *décimas* "Al toro que mató Felipe IV ("To the Bull that Philip IV killed"). His poem is neither better nor worse than those of his fellow poets. The same concepts, the same images, the same rhymes reappear inevitably in all poems.[19] The significance of the event is that Spain's greatest pens did not disdain such a eulogy. The incident offered them the opportunity to gain the king's attention; but lest the role of self-interest be too much stressed, it is well to remember that these poets probably took a Baroque pleasure in the elaborate embroidery of a trivial event.

Saavedra's best-known poem is the sonnet "Ludibria Mortis" ("Mockery of Death"), which closes his most famous book, *The Royal Politician*. The engraving that illustrates the poem shows a skull resting on stones which lie amidst fallen columns. Nearby on the ground are a crown and a sceptre. The theme, an old one in literature and art, to be sure, was especially dear to the Baroque artist. Saavedra's pictorial emblem brings to mind paintings by his younger contemporary Juan de Valdés Leal (1622? - 1690), who was working in Seville. At the behest of that reformed Don Juan, Don Miguel de Mañara (1626 - 1679), Valdés Leal did two paintings for the Hospital of Charity in Seville which elaborate on the same theme: *In Ictu Oculi* (*In the Twinkling of an Eye*) shows a skeleton extinguishing the light of life beneath the Latin words of the title while in his other arm he bears both a scythe and a coffin. At his feet lie the robes and crowns of bishop and prince.[20] The companion painting, *Finis Gloriae Mundi* (*The End of Worldly Glory*), shows the dust and skeletons of a bishop and a knight in coffins against a background of bones while above them vices and virtues are balanced on scales.

In the sonnet Saavedra directs himself to the princes and monarchs for whom he wrote his book. The skull belonged to a mortal ruler; now his crown has fallen. His smile no longer pleases; his frown inspires no fear. The final tercet calls for Christian humility:

> ¿Qué os arrogáis, ¡oh príncipes!, ¡oh reyes!
> Si en los ultrajes de la muerte fría
> Comunes sois con los demás mortales?

> (Can you be proud, oh princes, kings,
> If frigid death assaults your corpse
> And leaves you dust like mortals all?)

III   *The Ills of the Monarchy*

Saavedra Fajardo's talents were not poetic albeit he was and is one of the great masters of style in the Spanish language. Although contemporaries speak of his ardent and fiery temperament in negotiations, the disposition of his mind was intellectual, not lyric. At the end of December, 1630, he dated an essay which pointed to the direction his life and works would take in the next two decades. He wrote in Italian under the title *Indisposizione generale della monarchia di Spagna: sue cause e remedii* (*General Malady of the Spanish Monarchy: Its Causes and Cures*).[21] The concerns he revealed in this essay, written on the basis of his Roman experience, were those he was to express repeatedly in everything he wrote; the Spanish monarchy, beset by internal flaws, was pitted against a Europe inimical to the ideals that Spanish thinkers supported. Especially striking is the parallel between the ideas expressed in this tract and those in the essay "O subir o bajar" ("Either Rise or Fall") in *The Royal Politician*, published a decade later.

While Saavedra was in Madrid in 1631—the year Philip IV shot the bull and inspired such an outpouring of verse—he continued work on a treatise in two parts. One part was called *Introducciones a la política* (*Introduction to Political Science*), the other *Razón de Estado del Rey Católico Don Fernando* (*Statecraft of King Ferdinand the Catholic*). On February 1 he addressed himself to the Count-Duke of Olivares, who had expressed an interest in the two works. Saavedra sent him the first part of each, and in his note explained that if the count-duke should approve his enterprise he would undertake to complete it. Saavedra's intent was to dedicate the first treatise to Olivares and the second one, which dealt with Ferdinand the Catholic, to King Philip IV, who was the great-great-

great-grandson of Ferdinand of Aragon and Isabel of Castile, the founders of the modern Spanish state.

In his draft of a dedication, Saavedra confesses that he is presumptuous in his attempt to merit the attention of the count-duke. Nevertheless, he takes heart, he says, when he thinks that "the most expert pilot does not disdain the aid of a tiny needle which will show him the direction." [22] Here, Saavedra reveals that love of metaphor which later, in *The Royal Politician*, leads him to construct political essays on the basis of a figure of speech or an aphorism, a trite or a picturesque concept, a proverb or a concrete example.

Either Olivares did not give Saavedra the encouragement he expected or else the author's attention was diverted to more practical affairs, for Saavedra never finished either of the treatises. We have only two books of a projected five of *Introduction to Political Science*. The thirteen very brief chapters—scarcely more than long paragraphs, in truth—of *Statecraft of King Ferdinand the Catholic* barely cover the civil wars over the disputed succession of Isabel to the crown of Castile. The works remained in manuscript until they were published for the first time in Saavedra's collected works in the Biblioteca de Autores Españoles in the nineteenth century. Saavedra conceived of the two works as forming one whole, and he designated them respectively "First Part" and "Second Part." On a small scale, they correspond to the grander concept which he would later have of *The Royal Politician* and of *Corona gótica* (*Gothic Crown*). *Introduction to Political Science* expounds theory; *Statecraft of King Ferdinand the Catholic* may be described as "applied history."

In his *Introduction to Political Science* Saavedra follows Aristotle in his *Politics*; he has also used ideas of St. Thomas Aquinas on city government and has applied them to his own times. The result is a restatement of commonplaces of the age. He must have known and read many of the treatises current in his day and most particularly the Jesuit Juan de Mariana's Latin work *De Rege et Regis Institutione*, which has been translated into English under the title *The King and His Education*. [23] The book appeared in 1599 just before Saavedra went to Salamanca. Mariana defended the idea, not new to be sure, that a people subjected to tyranny had the right to kill the tyrant if they had exhausted every other means of defense. He condoned the crime of Jacques Clément, who had murdered Henri III of France in 1589, a recent event. When another assassin, Ravaillac, killed Henri IV in 1610—Saavedra was

in Rome at the time—Mariana was thought to be responsible, and
his book was solemnly burned in Paris. Saavedra wrote a chapter on
tyranny in his treatise, the last one in the manuscript he gave to
Olivares. However, he avoids the sensitive issue of tyrannicide, and
since the treatise ends at that point we do not know whether he intended to deal with the subject.

IV *Poetry and Politics*

The Portuguese man of letters Manuel de Faria e Sousa (1590 -
1649) gives us a curious insight into Saavedra's activities as a writer
and a bureaucrat in the 1630's. Faria e Sousa was some six years
younger than Saavedra. He served as a secretary in the household of
the Portuguese nobleman Dom Manuel de Moura Côrte Real,
Marquis of Castelo Rodrigo. At the time that Saavedra knew him,
Faria had published both verse and prose and was at work on the
monumental commentary on Camões's *Lusiads* which he was to
bring out in 1639.[24]

In the preceding century, Philip II, pressing his claims to the Portuguese crown, had added the neighboring country to his realms.
From 1581 until the successful rebellion of 1640 - 41, members of
the Portuguese nobility were accustomed to serve the Spanish
monarchs in government positions. Thus it happened that in 1631
the Marquis of Castelo Rodrigo was in Madrid preparing to go to
Rome, where he would replace Cardinal Gaspar de Borja,
Saavedra's long-time chief, as Spanish ambassador. Although
Saavedra had returned to Spain with the hope of staying—"I am
too old to return to Italy again," he wrote the king—he apparently
now expected to be sent back.[25] Reading between the lines of Faria
e Sousa's autobiography, we can guess that Borja and Saavedra
wanted to have influence among the staff members of the new ambassador. Although the marquis had brought Faria e Sousa from
Lisbon to Madrid with the promise that he would be the embassy
secretary, the nobleman gave in to the persuasion or the pressure of
Saavedra Fajardo, who was in Madrid in 1631, and named another
man, Francisco de Párraga y Rojas, to the secretaryship. He then
tried to make amends by calling Faria e Sousa his private secretary.

Saavedra intervened again in the new ambassador's ap-
pointments. This time it was evidently his intent to have Faria e
Sousa himself named cryptographic secretary. Saavedra invited
Faria to go for a ride with him in his carriage and directed that it be
driven to a spot, not far from the royal palace, which overlooked the

Manzanares River and the Casa del Campo, a royal hunting preserve. Faria writes in words that reveal the pique he felt and his dislike of Saavedra: "he kept on reciting his verses to me. He had begun as soon as we had started riding, because he takes pride in being a great poet, and he was doing me a favor in letting me listen to him. Then, turning his eyes toward the river and the Casa del Campo, which can be seen from the place we had stopped, he began praising the view, and then he said that all that was nothing compared with what was to be found in Rome, where there were things that only men like me could appreciate" (p. 217).

This passage from Faria's autobiography suggests that Saavedra was the author of more verse than has come down to us. Faria did not much esteem what he heard, and he was probably right if we are to judge by what has survived. However, Saavedra was using his verses as a means of ingratiating himself with the Portuguese poet and scholar. From poetry, the conversation turned to the embassy job, and Saavedra went on to extol the honor attached to the post of cryptographic secretary. Faria had evidently determined that if he could not be embassy secretary, he would remain in the private service of his master. That, at least, is what he wrote that he told Saavedra. He also guessed the latter's intent, which was to have his and Borja's own men as both embassy secretary and cryptographic secretary.

Faria accompanied the Marquis of Castelo Rodrigo in the voyage to Italy. The marquis and his retinue stopped in Genoa, and there they spent several months. Borja was engaged in a dispute with the Pope, and the Spanish government did not want to relieve him during the quarrel. Saavedra, returning to Italy from Spain, also appeared in Genoa. The marquis, again at Saavedra's urging, offered Faria the post of cryptographic secretary and again he refused to accept it (p. 262). According to Faria e Sousa, Saavedra expected to exercise more influence over the marquis than he did over Cardinal Borja, and he urged the nobleman to hasten his departure from Genoa to Rome (pp. 266 - 67). Since an ambassador ordinary was more esteemed and more powerful than an ambassador extraordinary, Saavedra proposed that Castelo Rodrigo present himself as the ordinary, "influenced by his own aspirations," says Faria e Sousa, "forgetting that he was the servant and creature of Cardinal Borja" (p. 280). Faria e Sousa detested Saavedra and paints an unflattering moral picture of the forty-eight-year-old diplomat: "This man stoops to meddling and craftiness in order to get his way. He says that every man holds in his own hands his good or ill fortune and that he must realize that the point is to advance his fortune even though the means be as abominable as wiliness and meddling." Then the Portuguese continues righteously: "If that is what he believes, he is wrong. A person is right who openly by legitimate acts, means, or agents tries to better his fortune. If he succeeds, he is blameless, though the other who stands in his way is not without blame" (p. 280).

While we cannot accept at face value the estimate of a man who obviously detested Saavedra, the assessment must nevertheless figure in our appraisal of Saavedra and his work. However, a document of this period gives us a different view of Saavedra's character. The Marquis of Castelo Rodrigo requested of him a statement about the conduct of affairs in Rome, and Saavedra prepared his "Noticias de la negociación de Roma" ("News of Roman Affairs"). The third paragraph could well fit into a moral treatise on the education of an ambassador:

People think that in Rome we need an ambassador who is false, cunning, and dissembling, a man who is lacking in credibility, trust, and probity. I should like the ambassador always to be cautious but not cunning, to be prudent, and nobly but judiciously candid. . . . If a man deceives others, everyone will try to deceive him. If a man is suspect to other people and lacks credibility, he cannot work with others. Truth is the surest weapon against deceit. Let the weak and skinny fox depend on astuteness and deception; the strong and generous lion will count on the respect which he inspires. Thus the ministers of a great monarch will leave to lesser princes those wiles which substitute for true power. My experience has taught me that in Rome respect for prudent and courageous virtue greatly facilitates the conduct of affairs.[26]

The moral posture which Saavedra took in *Introduction to Political Science*, and that he was to take in *The Royal Politician*, is confirmed in "News of Roman Affairs." Saavedra Fajardo learned practical politics in the diplomatic jungle of seventeenth-century Rome. He was to exercise his craft—Faria e Sousa would have said his craftiness—in some of the principal courts of Europe. When he recorded his wisdom, however—whether in a political treatise or a simple bureaucratic document—he did not lose sight of moral issues.

V *Practical Politics and Machiavellianism*

Saavedra Fajardo used the phrase "razón de estado" in the title of the second part of his dual treatise, *Introduction to Political Science and Statecraft of King Ferdinand the Catholic*. This expression was the most widely debated topic of the century in the art of government. Giovanni Botero published a famous book in 1596, four years before Saavedra went to Salamanca, under the title *Ragion di Stato*. The words have been rendered into English as either "statecraft" or "practical politics."

It is a matter of interest that Saavedra chose to discuss the statecraft of Ferdinand the Catholic. The Spanish monarch is said by some to have served equally with Cesare Borgia as a model for Machiavelli's *The Prince*; yet for seventeenth-century Spaniards Machiavellianism represented perfidious politics in opposition to the Christian statecraft which they advocated. Father Claudio Clemente published, first in Latin (1628) and then in Spanish (1637), *El maquiavelismo degollado por la cristiana sabiduría de España y Austria* (*Machiavellianism Beheaded by the Christian Wisdom of Spain and Austria*).

In modern times it has become fashionable to rehabilitate Machiavelli. Was it not his purpose, in the *Discourses*, to reform the present by seeking solutions in Livy, an ancient historian? Did he not seek to substitute something better for the corruption and failure that he observed in his own times?[27] Spaniards of the seventeenth century asked no such questions. They read and discussed the famous passage in Chapter XVIII of *The Prince* in which Machiavelli advises the sovereign to feign virtues if he does not possess them:

. . . it is well to seem merciful, faithful, humane, sincere, religious, and also to be so; but you must have the mind so disposed that when it is needful to be otherwise, you may be able to change to the opposite qualities. And it must be understood that a prince, and especially a new prince, cannot observe all those things which are considered good in men, being often obliged, in order to maintain the state, to act against faith, against charity, against humanity, and against religion. And, therefore, he must have a mind disposed to adapt itself according to the wind, and as the variations of fortune dictate, and, as I said before, not deviate from what is good, if possible, but be able to do evil if constrained.[28]

Spanish moralists paid little heed to Machiavelli's parenthetical qualification that it is also well to be virtuous and if possible not to deviate from the good. They could not leave unchallenged his blatant attack on Christian virtues. In his *Tratado del príncipe cristiano* (*Treatise on the Christian Prince*; 1595), Pedro de Ribadeneyra writes against "the stupid impiety and the impious stupidity of this unfortunate master of the politicans of our day. . . ."[29]

The Spanish attitude is understandable in the light of the times.

The defeat of the Spanish Armada by the English in 1588 marked a turning point in Spanish fortunes in Europe, but the prolonged and bitter Thirty-Years' War (1618 - 1648) was the nation's undoing. The period coincided with Saavedra's maturity and with his diplomatic career. Spain was pitted against the France of Richelieu and Mazarin; in the politics of the French, Spaniards saw Machiavellianism in action.

Yet the opposition to Machiavellianism had a deeper cause. The Florentine's entire work was a refutation of the divinely ordered universe in which Spaniards still fervently desired to believe. Machiavelli attacked the great bulwark of natural law which had so carefully been built up over the centuries. He eschewed a politics of faith. It is notable, for example, that despite the many citations which he brings into his works, he seldom employs Biblical sources. Not only did Machiavelli free politics from faith but he separated it from reason as it was understood by Christian writers, for he divorced reason from revealed morality. In his justification of the use of violence, force, and deceit, Machiavelli is advising the prince to resort to irrational methods, and Spanish writers point out that violence is an extreme which is out of consonance with man's rational nature.

In 1633 Saavedra was plunged into the violence that raged in central Europe. On February 26 the Spanish king resolved that Cardinal Borja be informed that he wished to send Saavedra to Germany as his representative. Spanish affairs in Bavaria had previously been handled through Spain's diplomtic mission in Vienna. The turn of events in central Europe required a Spanish diplomat at the court of Bavaria, and Saavedra was selected for this post. As a result, at the age of forty-nine Saavedra left Rome, where he had spent more than a quarter of a century, to embark on a series of diplomatic missions in the heart of war-ravaged Europe. The next dozen years, from 1633 to 1645, were to be the most active of his life; they were also his most productive as a writer.

Thus Saavedra was destined to play a larger role upon the European stage in the struggle between the Hapsburgs and Bourbon France. Cardinal Richelieu was determined that the dominions of His Most Christian Majesty the King of France should rival those of His Most Catholic Majesty the King of Spain. To this end he directed the diplomacy, the propaganda, and the armed might of France. In the march of history the Thirty-Years' War separated Hapsburg hegemony in Spain and central Europe before 1618 from French dominace after 1648. For Spain the debacle occurred with the Peace of Westphalia in 1648 and became conclusive with the Peace of the Pyrenees in 1659, after which the Infanta María Teresa married Louis XIV on an island in the Bidasoa River in 1660.

In the European politics of the 1630's it was important for Spain to maintain a line of communication between the north of Italy, where Spanish forces were deployed and staged, and the Spanish Netherlands (modern Belgium). Saavedra's assignment was in response to this necessity. In July of 1632 he himself had suggested in a letter to the count-duke that Spain should have a representative at the court of Maximilian I, Duke of Bavaria and an Elector of the Holy Roman Empire.[30] The instructions that he received in April of 1633 were, first, that he should keep the duke on good terms with Emperor Ferdinand II, who was the uncle of Philip IV; and, second, that he should determine what relations, if any, the duke had with France and keep the Spanish minister in Vienna informed of them.[31]

Saavedra was to travel to Bavaria by way of Milan. There Philip's brother, the Cardinal-Infante Fernando, was at the head of a Spanish army destined to go to the Netherlands. After conferring with him, Saavedra proceeded north through Lombardy along the shores of Lake Como and through the Valtelina, the long broad valley of the Adda River which is separated from the Swiss canton of Grisons by the Rhaetian Alps. In the preceding decade it had been the site of bitter fighting between Protestants and Catholics, and between France and Spain, and it had then become a protectorate of the Papacy, which permitted the passage of Spanish troops. In his letter to Philip IV Saavedra reported: "I set out through the Valtelina, observing at all times the disposition of the land and the passes of that valley which is so important for the security of the state of Milan and so essential for the aid of the Empire and Flanders."[32] It was summer when Saavedra arrived at the Bavarian court, which at the time was in the city of Braunau on the River Inn north of Salzburg. Good diplomat that he was, he immeditely distributed gifts, in particular to the duchess and her ladies-in-waiting. These, he says, were very well received "on account of the Germans' avaricious nature. . . ."[33] In turn the duchess presented him with six fine mares.

Bavaria was one of the most important of the German states. Its territory was traversed by two rivers, the Rhine and the Danube, one flowing to the west and the other to the east. Its duke, Maximilian I of Wittelsbach (1572 - 1651), belonged to a family, older than the Hapsburgs themselves, which had at one time occupied

the imperial throne. He had begun his reign in 1598 at the youthful
age of twenty-six. He vigorously supported the Counter-
Reformation and the Catholic League. Subject to him were ninety-
three counts, barons, and knights; thirty-four cities; and one-
hundred and four abbeys and monasteries. His capital was Munich,
which the Spaniards of that day called Mónaco, thus causing us to
confuse it with the Mediterranean principality of that name. The
city had close to 100,000 inhabitants. Maximilian had adorned it
with magnificent buildings and extensive gardens. Although
Saavedra first met the Bavarian court at Braunau, he followed it on
its return to Munich, which was at the crossroads of central Europe.
There he made his headquarters for the next several years, but his
missions took him into the neighboring regions, which had suffered
the devastation and pestilence of the religious wars. That very year
of 1633 the villagers of Oberammergau, southwest of Munich, took
a vow to perform a passion play every tenth year in gratitude for the
cessation of a plague, and in 1634 they put it on for the first time.

In the court at Munich Saavedra encountered a veritable hatred
for Wallenstein, the German duke, once in the service of the
Emperor, whose large army and wavering loyalties made him at
once formidable and unpredictable. Duke Maximilian, who felt
abandoned in the face of the Wallenstein threat, considered the pro-
tection offered by France better than that of Spain, which had made
advances to the general. To be certain, Maxmilian was pleased
with the presence in Alsace of a Spanish army under the Duke of
Feria. Furthermore, the Bavarian Elector, like his wife, was of a
grasping nature. Saavedra quickly recognized his weakness, and
sought foreign aid funds for him from Madrid. After considerable
negotiation Saavedra was authorized to pay the Bavarian duke ten
thousand ducats a month, and thenceforth he was more successful
in his plan to alienate the duke from the French.[34] A new set of
problems arose when Feria's army arrived to spend the winter of
1634 in Bavaria. The accommodations for the army were not
satisfactory, and Saavedra was charged with obtaining amelioration.
Then the Duke of Feria himself became ill and died, and had to be
replaced. On the other hand, the Bavarian peasants, recalling the
recent and cruel depredations of Wallenstein's soldiers when they
were quartered among them, became angered at the arrival of new
soldiers in their villages, and rose in revolt. Apparently they had
good reason, for the discipline of the soldiers in Spain's famed *tercios* was disintegrating as the Spaniards came in contact with the
undisciplined troops of the Emperor.[35]

Such were some of the problems that Saavedra had to face. He was accredited to the court of an avaricious prince, whose territory lay athwart an essential land route to the Spanish Netherlands. The diplomat often received conflicting orders from the Cardinal-Infante and from Madrid. He was in the middle of a fluctuating and often disintegrating military situation. Yet he appears in his letters enormously active and dynamic. His work did, in fact, attract attention in Madrid. In 1633 the Council of State observed that "up to now this minister has been proceeding with great understanding, skill, and intelligence."[36] The following year the Council recommended that the king thank Saavedra for the care and attention which he was giving to His Majesty's affairs. Saavedra even won the good will of Maximilian, who was so impressed by his ardent nature in negotiations that he wished to employ him in his own affairs.[37]

VI *1635*

The year 1635 saw the struggle between France and Spain renewed with increased intensity. The war of propaganda was waged with a ferocity no less devastating than the conflict on the field of battle.

In 1634 the priest Besian Arroy, a doctor of theology from the University of Paris, published a book entitled *Questions décidées sur la justice des armes des Rois de France . . . (Questions Answered on the Justice that Attends the Arms of the Kings of France . . .)*. It was widely circulated and was held to be the basis for Richelieu's plan of action. Arroy envisaged a new Pan-Gaulism founded on Charlemagne's empire: "The realm of Charlemagne and other predecessors of Louis the Just [that is, Louis XIII] consisted of France, Germany, Italy, part of Spain, etc. Therefore, Louis the Just ought to reign over this realm."[38] The duke of Bavaria could well be concerned at what he read in the book, for his domain had once belonged to Charlemagne's empire. Spaniards, too, had cause for alarm, for Father Arroy's interpretation of Charlemagne's incursion into Spain was such that he believed France had rights to Portugal (in 1634 a part of the Spanish monarchy), Castile, Aragon, and Catalonia—well over half of the Iberian peninsula.

The French aim was a monarchy in the West with Paris the capital (as there had been an Eastern empire with Byzantium the capital); the means of securing the objective was war. A just war, to be sure. Basing his arguments on the conditions set down by St. Thomas Aquinas for a just war (sovereign authority, righteous intention, and an honest motivation), Arroy proves the justice of the French cause. If the war itself is just, then the means are also justified; and thus may Machiavellianism be reconciled with the aims of the ministers of His Most Christian Majesty. Arroy even proves, among other points, that alliances with heretics are legitimate. This consorting with heretics was incomprehensible to seventeenth-century Spaniards, and their incomprehension was to prove one cause of their undoing.

Arroy's book was but a prelude to a real shocker in the propaganda war. On June 6, 1635, the French government issued, over the signature of Louis XIII, a document which in its Spanish version bore the title *Manifiesto del Rey de Francia sobre el rompimiento de la guerra con España* (*Declaraion of the King of France on the Outbreak of War with Spain*). The author was Father Joseph de Paris, a Capuchin friar and one of Richelieu's men. The tract made three principal points. It began by emphasizing "the jealousy and natural hatred" that Spaniards felt for the French. It presented France in the noble and glorious role of protecting its allies from Hapsburg ambitions. It put special emphasis on the position of Flanders, the oppressed land which, in the French view, served as a fortress from which Spanish arms harassed the heartland of France. Furthermore, the document described in detail favors that France had rendered Spain, and in contrast it listed those situations that showed Spain's determined enmity for France. In effect, the tract proved that France had just cause for war. "We hereby declare," the document proclaimed, ". . . that we have determined and resolved henceforth to wage open war on sea and land against the said King of Spain, his subjects, and vassals. . . ."[39]

The French declaration, accompanied by military action, produced a military response from Spain. The accusations contained in the document likewise resulted in a strong reaction from Spanish writers. Many were the pamphlets and even books that were written attacking France and defending Spain. Some were printed for the public, others circulated in manuscript within the Spanish government. Several of the writers were serious historians who relied on facts to confound the French and their sympathizers: Alonso Guillén de la Carrera, Gonzalo de Céspedes y Meneses, and José Pellicer y Tovar (the editor of the book of poems about the bull that Philip IV shot). Others leaned to polemics and propaganda. Among them were Francisco de Quevedo, Matías de Novoa, and Jerónimo Mascareñas. Whatever the tone of their writings, they stood for certain principles which they believed the French endangered: the defense of the faith, the maintenance of peace, the rule of law, the dynastic principle, moderation.

Europe, in bondage to the legacy of Machiavelli, was in the process of rigorously separating the sphere of politics from the sphere of morality. The process was justified by "razón de estado," by statecraft, by practical politics. In the long road of history the declaration of 1635 was an incident that pointed the way to French triumphs: the Peace of Westphalia of 1648 (the year Saavedra died), the Peace of the Pyrenees of 1659 which led to the marriage of María Teresa to Louis XIV, the War of the Spanish Succession (1700 - 1713), which secured for a Bourbon prince his rights to the Spanish throne. The final ignominy occurred a century later, after revolutionary France had become imperial France, when French troops occupied Spain and Joseph Bonaparte briefly sat on the Spanish throne, won for him by the deviousness of his brother Napoleon. To be sure, Napoleon himself was defeated by an alliance of most of Europe, but France had achieved her aim of centuries. Spain was crushed, and never again would pose a serious threat to France.

Saavedra Fajardo's contribution to the propaganda war of 1635 is a sixty-page pamphlet entitled *Respuesta al manifiesto de Francia* (*Answer to the French Declaration*), printed at Madrid by Francisco Martínez and sold in Domingo de Palacio's bookshop just off the Puerta del Sol. In it, Saavedra pretends to be a French gentleman, a ploy that he was to repeat on a later occasion. The subtitle reads: "A Memorial sent to His Most Christian Majesty by one of his most faithful vassals concerning the declaration of June 6 of this year of 1635 which deals with the outbreak of war against the King of Spain."[40] On folio 2, the supposed translator addresses the reader, stating that he has translated the pamphlet "from the French original which was written by a gentleman of that nation, a man of great parts and very well informed. . . ." Was there a French original? While it is logical to suppose there was, if the work was to have its full propaganda effect, a copy has not come to light. The Spanish pamphlet itself is extremely rare.

The supposed vassal of the king of France addresses his monarch, telling him he must conceal his name, for Frenchmen suffer the injustice and tyranny of Cardinal Richelieu out of fear of violent death. His purpose in writing, he says, is to tell the naked truth, and he establishes first the "undeniable principle that the worst and the greatest of all afflictions is war. . . ."[41] Saavedra's pacifism is based on reason: war is unreasonable and contrary to the nature of man. Hence, the best policy will be the one that successfully preserves peace and friendship among men.

On this point and on many others Saavedra seems to be in accord with the general line of thought of contemporary Spaniards. Yet we detect in this pamphlet the dualism which will be apparent in his major work, *The Royal Politician*. It is the contrast between the idealism of his anti-Machiavellian principles and the realistic outlook of the man of action. For example, as an idealist he envisages a Christian community of nations and a universal monarchy. Yet his practical work in international affairs is already leading him toward the concept of a balance of power among states, whether he likes the consequences or not. The pamphlet is not written in abstractions, however. It is a bold and forthright attack on Cardinal Richelieu and his policies. As a writer of propaganda, Saavedra was successful because he pretended to be a Frenchman, loyal to his monarch but critical of the prime minister. While he opposed Machiavellianism in both theory and practice, he himself was becoming adept in the arts of subversion.

VII   *The View from Central Europe*

Saavedra Fajardo spent seven years, from 1633 to 1640, assigned to the court of Bavaria. While he maintained his headquarters there he often left Munich on missions to other points in central Europe. In December, 1636, he was present, in the capacity of minister, at the Electoral College at Regensburg (Ratisbone), north of Munich, which chose Ferdinand III (1608 - 1657), King of Hungary and Bohemia and Archduke of Austria, as King of Germany, a step toward his becoming Holy Roman Emperor the next year when his father died.

At Regensburg Saavedra wrote his *Discurso sobre el estado presente de Europa* (*Discourse on the Present State of Europe*), which a modern Spanish diplomat, Manuel Fraga Iribarne, has called "a real masterpiece of cool and exact judgment."[42] The *Discourse* is dated January 20, 1637, a month after the election of the new king of Germany. It was intended for the Cardinal-Infante and the Count-Duke of Olivares, to each of whom Saavedra sent copies. The letters that accompany it are dated at Munich on March 12 and April 1, respectively. The manuscript in the National Library at Madrid is the deciphered copy of an encoded dispatch.[43]

This *Discourse* differs from Saavedra's works of propaganda of the same period. He is making an honest report to his superiors. He gives the facts as he sees them and his interpretation of them from the vantage of his position in central Europe. The wars had come to a temporary halt in May of 1635 when the Emperor, Ferdinand II, had signed the treaty of Prague with the Protestant princes who were disposed to lay down their arms. A month later Richelieu had opened the new phase, the French phase, which was to last until 1648. Saavedra sees no special advantage for Spain in the election at Regensburg. The aged Emperor and his inexperienced son are men of good intentions, but like his own Duke Maximilian, they want Spanish money without Spanish authority. After sketching the situation in both the German states and in northern Italy (where the Valtelina had fallen once again into French hands), Saavedra observes: "In this confusing and dangerous state of affairs, peace is what everyone needs" (p. 1325). The key to the present situation, however, is France. Richelieu, Saavedra wrote, "has brought on these wars [and] he feeds the flames of conflict because only thus can he keep himself in the good graces of his monarch" (p. 1325). The wily cardinal can count upon the Swedes and many of the German princes to keep up the fighting in Germany while France can turn her attention to the encircling dominions of the king of Spain. "The world cannot be set aright until either foreign arms or internal disturbances bring the strongest pressure to bear on France" (p. 1325). He concludes the *Discourse*, however, with an expression of faith in his own art of diplomacy: "Matters have reached such a point that not force alone but rather ingenuity can set them aright. We must employ both" (p. 1328).

The next year, 1638, was a busy one which began auspiciously for Saavedra. He traveled from the Bavarian court across Switzerland to the duchy of Mantua, which had but recently emerged from the War of the Mantuan Succession (1627 - 31). There, in March and April, he concluded an advantageous agreement with the regent, Maria Gonzaga, Princess of Mantua and Montferrat, mother of the young duke Charles II. The princess agreed to leave the French side and adhere to the side of the Spanish king and the house of Austria. In return, Spain offered financial and military aid.

From Mantua Saavedra went back through Switzerland, and this journey was the occasion for his writing another piece of propaganda: *Dispertador a los trece cantones de esguízaros* (*Warning to the Thirteen Swiss Cantons*), which bears the date 1638. We know it only through a manuscript in Spanish in the National Library at Madrid. It was printed in the nineteenth century and again in the *Complete Works* of 1946.[44] However, if it was to have the effect that Saavedra desired, it must have appeared in print in Switzerland. Since it is a short piece of some eighteen hundred words, we can imagine it as a broadside, an ephemeral sheet or pamphlet. We must imagine, too, that it was written in a language understandable to the Swiss, probably German, or French, or perhaps both. No printed copy, however, has been discovered.

In *Warning to the Thriteen Swiss Cantons*, Saavedra used a ploy similar to the one that he had devised for *Answer to the French Declaration* of 1635. He writes as if her were a Swiss addressing members of the Swiss Diet. The Swiss were leaning toward France. For the Spanish, Swiss neutrality was preferable to partiality for France if they could not hope for outright support. Hence, Saavedra urges the prudence of a neutral stance.

The significance of the document lies in Saavedra's willingness to compromise on the middle way. "I do not say that we should break our ancient agreements with the crown of France, nor make war," wrote Saavedra in the persona of a Swiss, "but, without reaching extremes, we should consult our own consciences, and we should bravely inform the French king that . . . we shall not permit him to blockade us by force of arms and that we are resolved to give him no more aid of men or provisions. . . ." (p. 1332). At the same time, he believes, so he writes, that the Swiss should come to the aid of one another or of any neighboring province—he is thinking of Franche-Comté—to preserve the existing *status quo.* "Our foreign aid policy is to preserve princes in their present boundaries, but not to help them seize other princes' territories" (p. 1332). *Warning to the Thirteen Swiss Cantons* closes with the fervent wish that the document "may awaken us in time from the error of our ways . . . and that we may recognize the danger which immediately threatens us . . ." (p. 1333).

During his trip back through Switzerland from Mantua, when it is to be supposed that he distributed the *Warning,* Saavedra was well received in the canton of Bern and was presented with a gift of wines which he in turn gave to the hospital. From Bern he traveled westward to Franche-Comté.

VIII   *The Mission to Franche-Comté*

The territory of Franche-Comté, known also as the county of Burgundy, belonged to the Spanish crown. It was bounded on the north by Lorraine, on the west by the duchy of Burgundy, on the south by Savoy, and on the east by Switzerland. Historically, it had belonged to the kingdom of Burgundy and later became the county of Burgundy as distinct from the duchy. It was a part of the inheritance of Charles V, and through him became a possession of the Spanish Hapsburgs. The capital was Dôle, which was only some eight leagues distant from Dijon, capital of the duchy of Burgundy. Charles V had built a strong fortification around Dôle in order to ward off repeated incursions by the French into his county of Burgundy.

Franche-Comté enjoyed political and social autonomy. The three estates were represented in its States General. Although the governor was appointed by the Spanish crown, he was a member of the nobility of Franche-Comté. The *Parlement* of Dôle served as both council of state and a supreme court, and its president and procurator general formed, with the governor, a ruling triumvirate. The University of Dôle provided the men who served in the States General and the *Parlement*. This oligarchy of men of superior birth and eduction was content to govern under the distant and benign aegis of the Spanish crown.

Although the county of Burgundy, that is, Franche-Comté, and the duchy of Burgundy had long been separated politically, geography made them mutually vulnerable. A treaty of neutrality was the logical solution, and it had been renewed repeatedly. Cardinal Richelieu was responsible for terminating the happy state of affairs that existed in Franche-Comté. He was concerned with the Spanish encirclement of France. In the seventeenth century France was almost completely surrounded by Hapsburg holdings. The Spanish Hapsburgs ruled not only the peninsula south of the Pyrenees but also the Flemish Netherlands to the north of France, the Franche-Comté to the east, and Milan in northern Italy. Their Austrian kinsmen, through the empire, maintained a shadowy control over the Rhenish provinces along the northeastern boundary. When Richelieu reopened hostilities in 1635, Franche-Comté was a primary target of his policy. However, in 1636 the capital city of Dôle had decisively resisted a French attack, thanks to the fortifications built by Charles V a century before.

Unfortunately, the very troops that were assembled to resist the French incursion—soldiers of Franche-Comté under the Marquess of Conflans, imperial troops under Matthias Gallas, and the troops of the duke of Lorraine—drained the resources of the county and then failed in an attempt to carry the war into the duchy. Richelieu mobilized an army under the duke of Longueville. At the same time, danger overtook the county from the north as that terrible soldier of fortune Bernhard, Duke of Saxe-Weimar (1604 - 1639), a

Protestant, threatened to invade with the intention of carving out a kingdom for himself. In the face of external dangers, the governor, the *Parlement*, and the duke of Lorraine found themselves at cross purposes and incapable of organizing a defense. The Cardinal-Infante, now in the Netherlands, ordered Saavedra to Franche-Comté to bring the conflicting parties together.

Saavedra wrote of his mission in his *Relación de la jornada al condado de Borgoña* (*A Journey to the County of Burgundy*).[45] It is addressed to Philip IV, and it is dated in Pontarlier, July 10, 1638, where he paused after his mission had been accomplished.

From Bern, Saavedra traveled north of Lake Neuchâtel and entered Franche-Comté at Pontarlier on the upper reaches of the River Doubs, which flows first northeast and then makes a great but irregular half circle to flow southwest through Besançon and Dôle. He stopped only briefly at Pontarlier, noting that the mountain region had suffered little war damage. He set out for Salins, and on entering the plain he encountered the devastation which he was to find thenceforth throughout the county:

. . . it is hard to imagine any misery that these vassals have not suffered, more due to friendly and auxiliary arms than to enemy forces. They live in the woods eating herbs and sometimes each other. In desperation they emerge to kill travelers so that it is impossible to travel except in a large convoy. Amidst such danger and confusion, commerce and culture have waned. The inhabitants can count no bordering land a certain friend, for their neighbors are either heretics or French. Even so, they are faithful vassals who, despite their wretchedness, deeply regret any change of rule (p. 1334).

At Salins, which furnished the crown with important revenues because of the tax on salt, Saavedra encouraged local officials to complete the fortifications they had begun and gave them four thousand francs to advance the task. But then in Besançon he encountered a situation that taxed his diplomatic skills. Besançon had the special status of an Imperial Free City which set it apart from the county of Burgundy. When Saavedra arrived, he found the city beset by pestilence, hunger, and political discord. The people and the government were at odds over a tax that had been imposed to strengthen the fortifications, and the protest was taking the form of tumultuous demonstrations. The leaders of the revolt were hotheaded youths, and it was rumored that the French were inciting them. The magistrates had resigned, but Saavedra persuaded them to withdraw their resignations until new elections could be held. He counseled them to pursue a soft line—"los medios suaves"—toward the rebellious youths, but he himself talked with the agitators and warned them that they must desist, for two enemy armies threatened the county and their city. If they did not cease their agitation, he bluntly told them, the Spanish king would punish them by confiscating their property and taking their lives.

Despite Saavedra's counsel, the magistrates placed the agitators under house arrest. This produced new tumult, just as the elections were being held on St. John's day, June 24. Crowds came to carry the arrested men to the polls in sedan chairs. Saavedra himself, mounted on horseback with other gentlemen of the city, endeavored to keep the peace so that the elections might be carried out in an orderly manner.

Three of the agitators were among twenty-eight citizens elected to choose the fourteen new magistrates. A fresh dispute arose over the election of a chairman, and the city was with no government at all for three days. Saavedra wrote the electors a letter begging them not to delay. Finally, the man chosen was François de Lisola—"a disturbed youth," according to Saavedra—whose sentiments were at that time thought to be pro-French.[46] One faction of the twenty-eight would not accept him as chairman, and he in turn refused to open the ballots that had been cast to elect the fourteen magistrates. Saavedra had to intervene again, and even after the fourteen were declared elected he was obliged to bring that group to their senses by again depicting the danger in which the city and Franche-Comté found themselves.

The account of the disturbances in Besançon is the most picturesque part of *A Journey to the County of Burgundy*. The rest of the document is interesting, however, for a variety of reasons. It gives us a firsthand account of the problems of governments and the sufferings of people in one of the many areas that were affected by events of the Thirty Years' War. It is filled with details that support the advice which the diplomat Saavedra offers to his monarch. We see in it the practical man of affairs who will translate his everyday experiences into the political theory of his masterpiece, *The Royal Politician*. Finally, Saavedra, writing in the heat of battle, expresses himself in that vivid and lucid language which he was to cultivate as one of the great stylists of the Spanish tongue. What we have before us is language far removed from the Baroque jargon of much seventeenth-century prose. Nor does it resemble either the diplomatic and bureaucratic cant of modern times and even less the simple-minded vacuity of contemporary journalism. It is rather the masterful account of an educated man in full possession of his native language.

IX   A Proposal to the Swiss

Having brought a modicum of harmony among the warring factions both in the county and in the Imperial Free City, Saavedra ended his mission in Franche-Comté with the expectation that the policy of neutrality would endure and that the cities were in a defensive posture. He returned to Switzerland, and, although his headquarters were still in Bavaria, during the next several years he concentrated his efforts largely in Switzerland. He had the official title of envoy plenipotentiary to the thirteen cantons as well as to the Imperial Diet of Regensburg. However, his Swiss credentials were repeatedly questioned because they were from the Cardinal-Infante rather than directly from the king of Spain. He established himself first in Fribourg, between Bern and Lausanne, at a point well within Switzerland but not distant from the border of Franche-Comté. The council of the canton authorized his residence there and presented him a welcoming gift consisting of a barrel of wine and six cheeses for himself and thirty bushels of oats for his horses. Saavedra could well consume the gifts, for he traveled with carriage, horses, and baggage, and a full retinue of servants.

Between February, 1639, and June, 1642, Saavedra attended meetings of eight Swiss Diets held in various parts of the country. He had several specific objectives. He had to maintain the right of free passage through Switzerland, which the Swiss had guaranteed in treaties of long standing. He hoped to restrict the recruitment of Swiss soldiers by the French; and, failing in that, since the French had treaty rights to recruit, he wanted to forbid the use of Swiss soldiers in the Low Countries against imperial troops. He pressed for the neutrality of both the cantons and Franche-Comté, and tried to have Swiss forces replace Spanish troops as garrisons in the fortified cities of Dôle, Gray, Salins, and Besançon, hoping thus to stay French aggression against them.

When Bernhard, duke of Saxe-Weimar, invaded the county of Burgundy, Saavedra urged the Swiss to defend the neutrality of Franche-Comté as well as their own. He put great ardor into the undertaking. The envoy of the Grand Duke of Tuscany reported in a dispatch of February 20, 1639: "Don Diego de Saavedra is traveling through the cantons like a madman crying: 'To arms, to arms!' in order to arouse the Swiss against Weimar."[47] Saavedra worked not only through the Diets. He also wrote anonymously to convince the Swiss that "it is not to their advantage to have the King of France as a neighbor as I have demonstrated in two books which, without the name of the author, I have distributed among them."[48] Unless Saavedra is calling *Warning to the Thirteen Swiss Cantons* a book, neither of these works has yet been included in the corpus of his known writings. On February 27, 1639, Saavedra attended the Diet of the Catholic cantons which met at Lucerne at the request of the Cardinal-Infante Fernando. There Saavedra presented his *Proposta fatta dal Sig. Don Diego Sciavedra alla Dieta de cantoni catolici in Lucerna (Proposal Made by Don Diego Saavedra to the Diet of Catholic Cantons in Lucerne)*. The tract has survived in its Italian redaction, which was sent to Cardinal Francesco Barberini, nephew of Pope Urban VIII. The Jesuit scholar Quintín Aldea, who published it, has detected in the Italian a strong Spanish flavor.[49]

Saavedra begins by emphasizing how important it is to the cause of Swiss neutrality that Franche-Comté lie between the cantons and the dynamic power of France. He lists the dangers that loom if France should occupy the intervening county of Burgundy. He conveys to the members of the Diet the concern of the Cardinal-Infante and the king of Spain for the security and independence of the Swiss cantons. To hold the French at bay, the Cardinal-Infante must cooperate with the Emperor and must enjoy the right of passage from Italy through Switzerland to Germany, and he must appeal to the Diet for men, supplies, and munitions to sustain the Spanish posture. The ultimate aim, he says, will be that the status of the several territories should revert to that which prevailed in 1634.

Despite his best efforts over a period of years Saavedra was destined to fail in his aims. The French were hard at work against him, and they repeatedly questioned his credentials and his right to make commitments. The minister of the House of Savoy wrote his government: "[Saavedra Fajardo] has failed, but it is not his fault. . . . The Spanish representative is an able and intelligent negotiator."[50] The years were strenuous ones. Once, he made a secret trip into Franche-Comté at considerable personal risk. He had to settle such vexing problems as reimbursing the government at Bern for excesses committed by Spanish troops. On the other hand, when a guard at the city gate of Bern made him pay fees despite his diplomatic status, he insisted on and received reimbursement. At the end of his fourth mission in 1642, Saavedra was fifty-eight years old, and he spent a vacation taking the baths at Pfäfers in the canton of St. Gall.

During the period of the Swiss negotiations Saavedra published at Munich, in 1640, his monumental book *The Royal Politician*, into which he distilled the wisdom acquired during a quarter of a century in Rome and seven active years in central Europe. The experiences and the book were to prepare him for his last great diplomatic assignment as a Spanish representative at the Congress for Universal Peace, held at Osnabrück and Münster, which brought to an end the Thirty Years' War.

CHAPTER 3

The Christian Prince

SAAVEDRA Fajardo dedicated his major work, *Idea de un príncipe político-cristiano (Concept of the Political-Christian Prince)*, published in English under the title *The Royal Politician* (1700), to the young heir of the Spanish Hapsburg dynasty, Prince Baltasar Carlos (1629 - 1646), the prince of Asturias. His birth had been the occasion for great rejoicing at the court and in the realms to which he was heir; and as the little prince grew, the expectations of his subjects were raised. We can see his portraits in the museums of the world, for Velázquez and other court artists painted him at different ages. In the Boston Museum of Fine Arts, the prince, accompanied by his dwarf, is shown at the age of two in 1631, wearing skirts of olive green velvet embroidered in gold with the warm red scarf of a military commander. In the Prado, we see him portrayed at the age of six, dressed for hunting in breeches and boots and bearing a miniature gun. Also in the Prado is that superb portrayal of the boy astride a prancing Andulusian mare. We see portraits of him on the walls of the Imperial Museum in Vienna and the Royal Museum in the Hague. In the Wallace Collection in London he is shown, again on horseback, as he practices at the riding school while a retinue of courtiers looks on. At the Prado again, we can see him as another painter, Juan Bautista Mazo, portrayed him a year before his death, a youth of sixteen dressed in black.

Baltasar Carlos was not quite eleven when Saavedra penned the dedication to him at Vienna on July 10, 1640. On the young prince were pinned the hopes of his people for the future of the Spanish monarchy. Saavedra's book, like a hundred or more others of the period, was devoted to instructing the prince or the monarch in the proper moral and political doctrines which he required for Christian rule in modern times.

I   *The Education of the Prince*

Saavedra's book belongs to a vast tradition of didactic writing
which has its roots in the very beginnings of literature itself. It also
possesses qualities peculiar to itself and to the age in which it was
written. Aristotle, to the extent that he was known in the Middle
Ages, had become an official part of Christian philosophy. The new
scholarship of the Renaissance had added a vast store of treatises on
moral and political philosophy from classical times. The new universities and the printing presses of the sixteenth century dis-
seminated to a wider audience than they had ever had the works of
Greek and Latin moralists, philosophers, and historians, thus
providing abundant sources of material to an age that relished the
support of authority. The Western heritage was not the only one.
Into the renewed stream of didactic literature from Greece and
Rome and into the Judeo-Christian patrimony, there flowed Oriental traditions. Spain, situated geographically and culturally at the
confluence of Christian and Arabic cultures, received, absorbed,
and then spread this vast Oriental literature. Like Aesop's fables, the
tales and apologues of the Orient provided the seasoning that made
moral philosophy palatable.

In the Spanish Middle Ages we find works that fuse the Indian
tale with the popular morality of the Occident. King Alfonso the
Wise (1221 - 1284) had a translation made from the Arabic of *Calila
e Dimna,* a book of Sanscrit origin. The title comes from the names
of two wolves, brothers, who are the protagonists of one part of the
work. A later version, frequently reprinted in the sixteenth century,
was entitled less picturesquely *Ejemplario contra los engaños y
peligros del mundo (Exemplar Against the Deceptions and Dangers
of the World;* 1493). Alfonso's nephew, Don Juan Manuel (1282 -
1349?), used it as a source for one of the most charming of medieval
books, *El Conde Lucanor (Count Lucanor).* The young and inexperienced count expresses a variety of doubts to his tutor Patronio,
who tells him a story that contains the solution to the corresponding
problem.

Spanish taste in literature has favored the didactic, and it has also
insisted that teaching be made pleasurable. The Horatian dictum of
mingling *utile dulci*—profit with pleasure—describes one of the
strongest currents of Spanish literature: "He has won every vote
who has blended profit and pleasure, at once delighting and instructing the reader." The Spanish writer ever wavers between the
emphasis implied in the word order of "enseñar deleitando" and

"deleitar enseñando." Thus the Spanish Middle Ages produced many works which represent an Oriental mold into which elements of classical philosophy and Christian morality have been fitted. From Arabic literature, for example, came the "mirror of princes," a kind of work designed for the moral education of the ruler. An example of its adaption into Spanish literature may be read in the second part of *La historia del Caballero Cifar* (*The Story of the Knight Cifar*; 14th century), in which the king of Mentón instructs Garfín and Roboán, the sons of Cifar.

A similar process occurred in works strictly Christian in nature. A book by St. Thomas Aquinas (1225? - 1274), *De Regimine Principum* (*On the Governance of Rulers*), was a handbook of Christian politics. It is a short, straightforward treatise in which moral philosophy is related to government as a part of the great medieval synthesis. Writers who borrowed their ideas from St. Thomas thought to make them more palatable, and hence more teachable, by citing examples to illustrate the point. The primary souces of examples are, to be sure, the Bible, the classical historians, and the Christian writers. However, a work can be made more delectable by the use of fiction, tales, and apologues. Oriental literature provided these in abundance, and works devoted to the education of princes became more literary and more creative. The Bachelor Alfonso de la Torre compiled the *Visión delectable de la philosophía e de las otras sciencias* (*Delectable View of Philosophy and of Other Sciences;* ca. 1440), an undigested encyclopedia of medieval knowledge, for the instruction of Prince Don Carlos de Viana, son of Juan II, king of Aragon and Navarre. Creative literature of the medieval period reflected similar concerns. The early novel of chivalry, *Amadís de Gaula,* especially in its last books, reveals an instructional intent related to that of the doctrinal treatises.

In the period from the fifteenth to the seventeenth century there was a growing realization on the part of the governed of the importance of the prince in the lives of his subjects. The king was no longer a petty chieftain in the manner of the Germanic kings. He was, beginning with Ferdinand and Isabel, a ruler whose domains were expanding through war, conquest, and marriage. His role became more and more exalted. It was vital that he be properly instructed in the moral and political philosophy of his times. Among the first books printed in Spain was Francisco Ximénez's *Régimen de príncipes* (*The Rule of Princes;* Valencia, 1484). The next two centuries saw a great flowering of didactic treatises on the subject by men whose names figure prominently in the history and literature of their day: Antonio de Guevara, Sebastián Fox Morcillo, Antonio Pérez, Pedro de Rivadeneira, Juan de Mariana, Juan Pablo Mártir Rizo, and Francisco de Quevedo, among many others.[2]

II   The Emblem and the Essay

The treatise on moral and political philosophy, straightforward in men like Rivadeneira and Mariana, developed an embellishment in the seventeenth century that is characteristic of the Baroque age. In the sixteenth century the Italian jurist Andrea Alciati (1492 - 1550) published his *Emblemata (Emblems;* 1552), a collection of moral lessons in Latin verse. Each emblem had a graphic representation with a poetic commentary. Alciati dealt with general morality, but he frequently applied the doctrine to the prince. He took his materials from apologues and from classical mythology, and a poetic tendency served to disguise the moral theme.

Alciati's *Emblems* were popular all over Europe and were widely translated and imitated. In Spain, the Salamancan professor Francisco Sánchez de las Brozas wrote erudite commentaries on them. Juan de Orozco y Covarrubias, brother of the lexicographer Sebastián de Covarrubias y Orozco—the brothers inverted their surnames—imitated Alciati in his *Emblemas morales (Moral Emblems;* 1591), but he accentuated the religious character. Hernando de Soto conserved the literary tone and the human value of the Italian's work in his *Emblemas moralizadas (Moralized Emblems* 1599). In both of these books the graphic representation is accompanied by a poem of eight verses. They were published in the decade when Saavedra was a schoolboy in Murcia just just before he went to Salamanca, and they had been in print for more than forty years when he published his own work.

What Saavedra Fajardo did in the *The Royal Politician* was to fuse the emblem with the treatise for the instruction of the prince. The idea was not original with him. In Cologne Jacob Bruck, called Angermunt, had already done so in his *Emblemata Politica (Political Emblems;* 1618). That Saavedra knew this work is unquestionable, for in some cases there is an absolute identity of unusual symbols. However, he himself had shown an early propensity toward this mode of expression, for some of the poems he wrote on the death of Queen Margaret in 1611 were glosses of the symbolic figures on the mausoleum dedicated to her. In *The Royal Politician,* however, Saavedra modifies the emblem in one notable way. In earlier books the graphic representation dominated, and the literary commentary on it, which was in verse, was slight. In Saavedra's major work, however, the graphic element serves only as a point of departure for an essay on a moral or political theme. Yet even in Saavedra the graphic image still had an importance that modern editions of *The Royal Politician* fail to convey. The engraving was attractively executed and contributed significantly to the purpose of delighting while instructing.

The emblem was, indeed, in perfect accord with the literary taste of the times. It came to be considered a literary genre as permanent as the epic or the drama, and as such it had its historians and preceptists. Juan de Orozco y Covarrubias, in the introduction to his own *Moral Emblems*, sought its historical antecedents, defined it, and fixed its rules. His brother Sebastián gave this definition in his thesaurus: "Metaphorically, the verses which accompany a picture or engraving are called emblems, by which we mean a concept that is moral or amorous or that refers to war or something similar, and which contributes to understanding the intent of the graphic image and of its author. This name is often confused with symbol, hieroglyph, pegma [an inscription], essay, insignia, enigma, etc."[3]

Sebastián then refers the reader to his brother's work. Juan makes distinctions among several words, including device *(devisa)*, essay *(empresa)*, and emblem *(emblema)*. The device, of chivalric origin, was an abbreviated representation of something the knight had done; it served to distinguish him from other knights. The essay *(empresa)*, on the other hand, was something he proposed to do. These terms are of interest because of the last words of the full title of Saavedra's book: *Idea . . . representada en cien empresas (Concept . . . Pictured in One Hundred Essays)*. The essay *(empresa)*—that is, the attempt, the enterprise, the objective to be realized—is, according to Juan de Orozco y Covarrubias, "the representation of some plan which, because it shows the aim of what is being undertaken, came to be called an essay." An emblem *(emblema)* is a "picture that means advice in the form of one or several representations."[4] Thus, to Juan de Orozco, writing in 1591, the *empresa* represented a purpose, while the *emblema* represented counsel or advice. Later, in seventeenth-century practice, the two came to be used without distinction. Both were to have a picture and a maxim. The picture was not to be so obvious that anyone could understand it nor so obscure that it was impossible to decipher. It should be pleasant to look at. The maxim was to contain a good moral and to be expressed succinctly and ingeniously. Neither should lend itself to a distorted interpretation.

It becomes apparent that the *empresa* and the *emblema* are the Baroque version of what we term today the essay. *Discurso*, or discourse, though widely employed, did not as a name have the special literary texture of *empresa* or *emblema;* the word *ensayo*, which also meant an effort or attempt, was not used then, and indeed not until modern times, to designate the interpretative literary composition.

The emblem was admirably adapted to the method of thought most suited to the age, namely the gloss. Two distinguished moralists of an earlier generation, Pedro de Rivadeneira and Juan de Mariana, divided their works into chapters by means of a logical organization. But in the seventeenth century there was an aversion to chapters. In the narratives of the time we find that Vicente Espinel used *descansos* (rest periods), Suárez de Figueroa *alivios* (alleviations,) Vélez de Guevara *trancos* (strides), and Gracián *crisis* (criticisms).[5] The emblem enabled the writer to make his internal division through isolated concepts; he did not necessarily follow a systematic development of his material. The emblem and the *empresa* fall clearly within the concept of the Baroque. Thought does not develop along a continuous internal line. It receives its initial impulse from an isolated concrete motif. The line is broken or disappears in the effort to give a greater expression of vivacity. This does not mean that an author has no basic lines of thought. It only signifies that his ideas must be sought throughout his work and pieced together coherently. To be sure, trains of thought may be left undeveloped. That did not bother the writer, however. To him it was important to present his material artistically so that it would be more efficacious. Thus, a treatise on government was properly a work of art, just as government itself was an art.

In the Spanish Baroque period there is a strong current of symbolism which is evident in the desire of writers to express one thing in terms of another. Writers search for the concrete expression which goes beyond the simple figure of speech to an absolute identification of the abstract and the concrete. In the Gongoristic technique the sparkle of the eyes *is* a diamond. The tendency was not confined to poetry. The literature of emblems brought symbolism to the formal treatise as the basic method for the elaboration of an idea. The reason for this development lay in an essential problem of the seventeenth century. Man, depraved by nature, is yet capable of reform. He can be impressed, and the impression must be made as ineradicable as possible; for man's will is naturally inclined toward evil, which is conceived of as more seductive than good. Therefore, truth must be so embellished that it will prove more attractive than evil and so clothed that it will make a lasting impression. The will was to be educated through an appeal to the senses. The medium was found in the emblem, which is both concrete and engaging.

The concreteness of the pictorial representation carried over into the written gloss which expatiated upon it. The example became the standard technique for the development of an idea as it was and survives today in sermons. The possibilities were truly endless, but one may suffice. For centuries the animal had served to teach man the way of morality. Animals belonged to that great book of nature in which man could read. They had, as Saavedra says with many others, been created for men's service (*Idea*, IV, 219).[6] For there was no doubt in the mind of the seventeenth-century man but that the world and its contents had been created for him: its main function was to provide symbols and to point morals for the benefit of man. The ant and the bee and the elephant were there for man to learn from. As Father Tomás Muniessa pointed out in the approbation of Francisco Garau's *El sabio instruido de la naturaleza (The Wise Man Instructed by Nature;* 1677), animals lacked reason and could not teach, but man could learn from them.[7] Saavedra says that "we have learned more about living from animals than we have from men."[8]

Besides the fables of antiquity and the animal apologues from the Orient, the seventeenth century had a wonderful additional source of material on animals in Luis de Granada's *Introducción al símbolo de la fe (Introduction to the Symbol of the Faith;* 1582) which suggested many an idea to the writers of emblems. Saavedra Fajardo often uses nature's creatures as symbols. For example, from the humble ant or the bee the great prince can learn to be provident (*Idea*, III, 226). In keeping with the anti-intellectual tone of *Republic of Letters*, he prefers that man read in the book of nature rather than in the books of scholars, for God has given nature to man for his instruction. Like Shakespeare's Jaques in *As You Like It*, the seventeenth-century man found "tongues in trees, books in the running brooks, sermons in stones," and a moral lesson in the animal world. Therein the writer of emblems found an abundant source of concrete examples for a symbolic expression.

III   A Sample Essay

It is not easy to grasp the nature of a Baroque essay by reading about it. One needs to experience it directly. Following in translation is a substantial part of one of Saavedra's essays. It is *empresa* number LX, which has something to say to the modern reader. The emblem or symbol is an arrow pointed skyward, and the title is "O subir o bajar" ("Either Rise or Fall"). It is one of the few titles in Spanish; most are in Latin, for the people of those days preferred their aphorisms in a classical language. In marginal notes Saavedra gave the sources for his ideas, and these are here shown in brackets, although the text is not encumbered with exact details of the citation.

EITHER RISE OR FALL

The arrow shot from the bow either rises or falls; it does not remain suspended in the air. It is like time, which slips into the past while it is still future; it is like the angles of a circle which pass from acute to obtuse without stopping at a right angle. The apogee of the arrow is also the point of its first declination. The higher anything rises, the nearer it is to falling. As soon as things reach their final state, they must inevitably start to decline. Hippocrates observed this fact in human bodies; when they can no longer improve, they do not remain stable but begin to deteriorate. Nothing is permanent in nature. The second causes of the heavens do not cease to operate, nor does the effect which they have on other things. To this fact Socrates attributed the changes that occur in republics [Aristotle]. Monarchies are not different from living creatures or plants. Like them, they are born, they live, and they die without any fixed age. Therefore, their fall is natural [Cicero]. If they do not grow, they diminish. Nothing can prevent a decline from the greatest good fortune. Once the monarchy has begun to fall, it is nearly impossible to stop it. It is harder for the majesty of a king to descend from the highest degree to a medium one than from a middle degree to the lowest [Livy]. But monarchies do not rise and fall at an equal pace, because the very elements of their grandeur are a weight which carries them downward at a greater speed as they seek the stability of a middle position [Seneca]. Alexander created his monarchy in twelve years, but it fell in less time, divided first into four kingdoms and later into several more.

Many are the causes of the rise and fall of monarchies and republics. He who attributes them to chance, or to the movement and influence of the stars, or to Plato's numbers, or to climacteric years, denies the concern of divine Providence for the things of this world. God did not disdain to create these orbs, nor does He disdain the governance of them, for to create something and then not care for it would negate the action itself. If God does not trust the brushes of others to illuminate the peacock's feathers or paint the butterfly's wings, can we believe that He leaves to chance the fate of empires and monarchies on which depend the happiness or grief, the very life or death of man for whom He created all things? It would be impiety on our part to believe so; it would be pride to attribute the course of events to our wisdom alone. Kings reign through Him; by His hand are scepters granted. Although He lets man's inclinations, whether innate or learned, influence the preservation or the loss of kingdoms, He works through man's free will, without encroaching on his freedom, to dispose through him the rise or fall of monarchies. So it is that no kingdom has been lost unless human imprudence or blind passions have intervened in the process [Sallust]. I almost dare to say that empires would endure forever if the ruler's free will balanced his exercise of power and if he brought his reason to bear on particular situations.

Since human prudence and judgment influence the decline of empires, we can readily demonstrate the causes of decline. Many are the general reasons that affect all kingdoms, whether acquired by succession, by election, or by the sword; but they can all be reduced to four sources from which all the other causes arise, just as the four principal winds produce many collateral ones on the earth's surface. These four causes are religion, honor, life, and property. For the purpose of preserving them, civil association was introduced, and people subjected themselves to being governed by one, by a few, or by many. Therefore, when people see that one of those four concerns is endangered, they rise up and change the form of their government. We shall touch on each concern briefly as befits the length of this essay.

Although religion is a unifying bond in the state, if there is not a single religion, it can cause more dissension than any other factor and bring down any of several forms of government. There cannot be peace and concord among those who have different beliefs about God, for if diversity in manners and dress produces dissension, what will not be the effect of different views concerning the Author of creation, what rage will not be engendered among those with different views on so important a subject? Freedom of conscience is the ruin of a state. In matters of religion the state has no need, as the Holy Scripture says, for a prick in the eye or a thorn in the side [Numbers 33.55]. The duties of fealty and the strongest ties of kinship and friendship are set at odds or broken entirely in order to preserve religious belief. The Spanish Gothic king Witerico [603 - 609 A.D.] was killed by his subjects because he tried to introduce Arianism into his kingdom. The same thing happened to King Witiza [701 - 709 A.D.] because he changed the customs and rites of worship. Galicia rose up against King Fruela I [757 - 768] because of the abuse of clerical marriage [Mariana]. As soon as different religions were permitted in the Netherlands, people began to disobey their natural prince.

Honor too, while it protects and preserves republics and enjoins loyalty, causes disturbances when people defend themselves from shame brought on by a slight, an offense, or an injury; for subjects place honor above property or life [Aristotle]. Count Julián brought the Africans to Spain when he found out that King Roderick had blemished the honor of his daughter Florinda. The *hidalgos* of Castile took up arms against King Alfonso III because he tried to infringe upon their prerogatives by forcing them to pay taxes as if they were plebeians. The subjects of Ramiro III, king of León, could not tolerate his harsh and arrogant treatment of them and they rebelled against him. The affronts which subjects receive incite them to seek vengeance against their prince [Aristotle], whether the prince feels it toward his subjects or they toward him, when he does not have the characteristics or qualities worthy of a prince, and his subjects think it infamous to obey a man who cannot command or make himself respected and who neglects his government.

The vassals of King Juan I of Aragon rebelled because he did not attend to his business; and likewise, in the case of the vassals of King Juan II of Castile, because he was inept in the exercise of power; likewise, the subjects of King Enrique IV, because of his vices and his lack of decorum and authority; likewise; those of King Alfonso V of Portugal, because he let himself be ruled by others. Subjects feel themselves no less aggrieved and belittled when they are ruled by foreigners, or when high offices and favors are distributed among outsiders; because, as King Enrique said, "it is equivalent to saying that in our kingdoms there is a lack of able worthy persons" [Revised Code of Law]. That was the cause of the rebellions in Castile in the time of the Emperor Charles V. The same thing happens when honors are ill distributed, because men of temperament cannot tolerate such a situation: they consider it a rebuff if others of less merit are preferred over them [Aristotle].

The greatest infirmity of a republic is incontinence and lasciviousness. From these vices are born sedition, the downfall of kingdoms, and the ruin of princes, for they blemish the honor of many other men, and God punishes them severely. Because of a single lecherous act, Spain was buried in ashes for seven centuries. Because of lechery Egypt repeatedly endured plagues [Genesis 12.17], and David and his descendants suffered many tribulations, for the sword never departed from his house [II Samuel 12.10]. It is no less a danger to the republic if many men are excluded from positions in the government, because they become enemies of the state, for no man is so low that he does not covet honor and resent being deprived of it [Aristotle]. This is a danger incurred by those republics in which a certain number of nobles enjoy power while the rest are excluded from it.

The third reason for rebellions and uprisings in kingdoms is for the purpose of preserving life when the subjects consider their prince so weak and cowardly that he cannot defend them; or when they despise him because of his severity, like King Alfonso X, or because of his cruelty, like King Pedro the Cruel; or when they consider him unjust and tyrannical in his actions so that the life of everyone is endangered, as occurred in the case of King Orduño II [914 - 924 A.D.], who infamously killed the counts of Castile, as a result of which action the government was changed [Mariana].

The last cause of rebellion is property. For example, the prince may consume that of his vassals; that was why García, King of Galicia, lost his kingdom and his life. Or the prince may prodigally waste the royal income; that was the pretext that Ramón used to kill his brother Sancho, King of Navarre. Or the prince may be avaricious, like King Alfonso the Wise. Or because of his mismanagement, people are in need, prices go up, and commerce and business decline; these were reasons that also made King Alfonso the Wise odious. Or the currency is unstable, as it was in the time of King Pedro II of Aragon and in the reigns of many other kings. Or jobs and wealth are ill distributed, for envy and need cause men to take up arms against the rich and result in sedition [Aristotle]. Sedition may also be brought on by the improper administration of justice, by the quartering of troops in citizens' homes, and by other demands upon the income and property of the king's vassals.

. . . .

I shall close this subject with two warnings. The first is that republics endure when they are either far removed from those causes which bring on their demise or when they are very near them. Over-confidence is dangerous, but fearfulness is solicitous and vigilant. The second warning is that neither in the person of the prince nor in the body of the republic should the slightest inroads or impairments be overlooked, for little by little they grow unnoticed until they can no longer be corrected [Aristotle]. A tiny worm eats away at the heart of a cedar tree and fells it. A little fish can stop a ship that is well favored by the winds. The more powerful the ship is and the greater its speed, the more easily is it undone by anything it strikes.

Slight losses brought on the ruin of the Roman monarchy. An indisposition may be more serious than a grave illness because one is neglected and the other gets attention. We try to cure a fever at once, but we ignore a discharge from the lungs, which usually develops into a more critical ailment.

IV   *From the Cradle to the Grave*

The abrupt ending, such as that of "Either Rise or Fall," occurs frequently in these essays. Sometimes, however, Saavedra brings the reader back to the original motif from which he departed. This technique gives the essay a more rounded and a more pleasing form. Even without such a conclusion, the essay possesses an underlying logic, once it departs from the generating motif, even though a train of thought may be obscured by ornamention, especially in the form of example.

The Royal Politician as a whole is not without a structure of its own; it is more than a series of disconnected essays. The 101 *empresas* (contrary to the subtitle there are 101 essays rather than one hundred in editions after the first) plus the final poem take the prince from the cradle to the grave.[9] The emblem of the first essay, "Hinc labor et virtus" ("Hence Toil and Courage"), shows Heracles in the cradle strangling the two snakes which Hera sent to kill him. The emblem for the final sonnet, entitled "Ludibria mortis" ("The Mockery of Death"), shows the scepter and crown lying on the ground beside broken columns while a skull rests on a cracked pedestal.

The 101 essays are grouped into eight sections. The first group of six essays deals with the youth of the prince and with his upbringing; the last two essays deal with his old age. The six sections in between are devoted to the reign of the mature monarch. They are a guide to the prince in his acts as man and monarch (Essays 7 - 37); they tell him how he is to deal with his subjects, with foreigners (38 - 48), and with his ministers (49 - 58); what his conduct should be in governing his states in normal times (59 - 72) and in periods of internal or external conflict (73 - 95); and what he should do at the moment of victory or in drawing up a treaty of peace (96 - 99). Each section of the book thus has a general subject, a theme, or an idea, around which the essays are clustered, but the approach in individual essays is by way of the graphic image and the aphoristic title.

In the first group of essays (1 - 6) on the upbringing of the young prince Saavedra expounds the theory of the *tabula rasa* (blank page) which John Locke (1632 - 1704) was to popularize. In "Robur et Decus" ("Strength and Honor") he emphasizes physical training, and in the next essay, "Non Solum Armis" ("Not by Arms Alone"), he stresses the importance of a knowledge of the arts and sciences. Learning, he says in "Deleitando enseñan" ("They Teach by Pleasing"), ought to bring delight, and it should be adorned with erudition.

In the largest group of essays (7 - 37), thirty-one in all, Saavedra counsels the prince on his general conduct as a human being and as a ruler. The prince should see things as they are, not as his passions may deform them. He must not let anger overpower reason, nor envy unseat the dominion of the intellect. He should be cautious in his use of words; he should encourage truth to overcome falsehood, for he may be certain that his defects will be the subject of gossip, which will give him warning of his faults. He ought to esteem his good name more than his life. He should compare his acts with those of his ancestors but must not be content with inherited glory. He should recognize God as the source of his scepter, with the knowledge that a successor will replace him, for his possession of the crown is but temporary. He should rule by law, affirming his majesty through justice and clemency. He must reward courage fairly. He should be guided always by the true faith, trusting to it the safety of his dominions; he should place his hopes of victory in true religion, not in false ones. He should consult times past as well as the present, studying not exceptional cases that will not likely occur again but rather those experiences of many people which serve to fortify wisdom. The experience of others will teach him to sustain his crown through the esteem in which he is held, but he must not depend on the opinion of the common herd. He must learn to put on a good countenance in the face of propitious fortune or bad, to suffer and wait, to shape adversity to his own advantage, to sail with a contrary wind, and to choose the lesser of two dangers.

In the essays that counsel the prince on his relations with his own subjects and with foreigners (38 - 48), Saavedra advises him to make himself both loved and feared by all. He should listen to the entreaties of everyone. He should temper force with generosity. He should avoid extremes and seek a middle way. He should recognize that his own fantasy may decieve him at the same time that he is wary of those who feign virtue or who ingratiate themselves with him through flattery and adulation.

This series contains two of the most controversial essays of the book. Essays XLIII and XLIV deal with dissimulation. The title of "Ut Sciat Regnare" ("In Order to Reign") is derived from the motto that Louis XI of France taught his son Charles VIII: "Qui nescit dissimulare, nescit regnare" ("He who does not know how to dissimulate, does not know how to reign"). The emblem of "Nec a Quo nec ad Quem" ("Neither Where nor Whom") is the snake. The title is derived from the Book of John 3.8, in which the subject is the wind, not a snake: "The wind bloweth where it listeth, and thou hearest the sound thereof, but canst not tell whence it cometh, and whither it goeth. . . ." Saavedra begins the essay with these words: "Ambiguous is the track of the snake which twists from side to side with such uncertainty that its own body does not know where its head will lead it. It signals a turn in one direction and moves in the opposite, and its passage leaves no mark nor can the intent of its journey be apprehended. The designs and intentions of princes ought to be in like manner concealed." Saavedra treads dangerously close to the practical politics of Machiavellianism; he comes close to counseling the very conduct on the part of his prince which he decries in others. These two essays thus lie at the heart of the grand problems of the age, to which we must later return.

In the series of ten essays (49 - 58) in which he explores the relationship of the prince with his ministers, Saavedra begins by emphasizing that their authority derives only from the prince. He should keep them subjected equally to his favor or his displeasure. Evil ministers are the more dangerous the higher the posts they hold. They feed their avarice on the high positions they occupy, and they long to act independently of their prince. But if counselors and

secretaries keep their place and do their job properly, then the
prince should reward them with honors that do not detract from his
position.

To the governance of the state under normal circumstances
Saavedra devotes fourteen essays (59 - 72). The series begins with
"Col senno e con la mano" ("With Judgment and Skill"), an Italian
phrase, which advises the prince that to acquire and to preserve his
states he must exercise both good sense and strength; for—this is
the essay "Either Rise or Fall"—a state must either grow or decline.
The state is likened to the harp: the prince must know its strings
and make certain that the highest and the lowest sound in harmony.
He should take time and consideration to reach a decision and then
should be quick to act. He should correct errors before they multi-
ply. On a practical level, he must be sure his lands are populated
and that from the populace he selects men interested in government. He must not burden his subjects with taxes. He should
promote trade and commerce. He should encourage hard
work—the title is, of course, "Labor Omnia Vincit" ("Work Con-
quers All Things")—which must be alleviated by decent repose. He
should become the master of war and peace through the power of
the sword and the purse.

Twenty-three essays (73 - 95) counsel the prince on his conduct
when his kingdom falls upon evil times, whether due to external or
internal causes. Internal sedition must be overcome quickly and
through the use of divisive tactics. War may properly be waged in
order to impose peace, but the prince who sows discord invites war.
War may also be instigated by the evil intentions of ministers—Richelieu is Saavedra's target, of course—or by rivalry among
princes. They disguise their true intentions so that their designs
must be countered through ingenuity. Weapons must be prepared
in advance, and the level of armed forces must be measured against
those of possible enemies. The exercise of arms must be esteemed,
for the preservation of the state depends on its armed strength,
although judgment ought to be exercised more than force. If the
country is at war, the prince should encourage his armies with his
presence. (Saavedra's own monarch Felipe IV roused himself from
his lethargy to accompany his armies to Catalonia in 1644 during
the war with France. Velázquez painted him at Fraga in his silver
and salmon uniform, a picture we can see today in the Frick Collection in New York. Was Felipe with his army on the advice of *The
Royal Politician*, which had been published four years before?) The
prince should bear in mind that his arms will be successful if God is

on his side, that concord is a powerful weapon, that diversion is a cunning tactic, that reconciled enemies are not to be trusted, that alliances with heretics are dangerous, that the Pope must be impartial, but that neutrality on the part of the prince will neither keep friends nor win over enemies.

In essays 96 - 99 Saavedra supposes that the prince has been victorious in conflict. He advises that in time of victory the memory of adverse fortune should remain alive. The victor should become stronger with the spoils. For the fruits of war should bring the sweetness of peace. In his closing essays (100 - 101) and in the poem Saavedra counsels that the last acts of a prince are those which crown his government and point to the future Finally, like the painter Valdés Leal, he reminds the prince that in death he is the equal of his lowest vassal.

Thus Saavedra has carried the prince—the Christian prince, let it be emphasized—from the cradle to the grave. So bare a summary of the contents might tend to confirm the judgment of Menéndez y Pelayo, who held *Republic of Letters* in high esteem. However, that critic called *The Royal Politician* a "long repertoire of commonplace ideas on politics and morality which is mighty hard to read in its entirety."[10] Yet on almost every page we detect the anguished question of that troubled age: Can Christianity and practical politics be reconciled? In their answers Saavedra and his fellow political writers attempted one of the great syntheses of the Counter-Reformation in Spain.

V   *Hic et Nunc*

The synthesis that Saavedra attempted was a noble aspiration that collapsed before the onslaught of modern pragmatic politics. Saavedra's agony nevertheless stirred the soul of a great twentieth-century Spaniard, José Martínez Ruiz, "Azorín," whose criticism reestablished Saavedra's position in Spanish letters. Azorín, who as an anguished youth witnessed the debacle of 1898, found solace in the experience of the aging diplomat who struggled to mitigate the humiliations in the offing in 1648, for the Peace of Westphalia confirmed Spain's continued decline which had begun sixty years before with the defeat of the Armada.

The pages of *The Royal Politician* are replete with citations from ancient and modern authorities. Aristotle, Plato, Sallust, Livy, Cicero, books of the Old Testament, Father Mariana—Greek philosophers, the Bible, Roman and Spanish historians—these are the sources for Saavedra's ideas in the single essay "Either Rise or

Fall." Saavedra was, however, very much a man of his times. He lived and worked close to a quarter of a century at the seat of Christendom, and he spent a decade in the heart of central Europe during the Thirty Years' War. In *The Royal Politician* he wrote pages that exude the reality of eyewitness accounts. The contrast between the ideal of his authorities and the world of his own day produces the agony of his book.

When we read the essay "Either Rise or Fall," we are struck by how much of what Saavedra says is applicable to our times. Occasionally, a jarring note occurs: he speaks of the quartering of the troops in citizens' homes. This was an abuse in his day, and we have much evidence of it in literature: Calderón's *El alcalde de Zalamea* (*The Mayor of Zalamea*), probably written between 1640 and 1644, is a famous example in Spanish literature. Nowadays, in most countries, the citizen is free of this oppression. But what of all the other evils that rulers and governments visit upon their "subjects": the manipulation of the currency, the waste of the public purse, the appointment of cronies to high office, excessive taxation, and so on and on? They are still with us everywhere.

There is much book learning in the *The Royal Politician*, but Saavedra selected what he included on the basis of his experience of reality and his understanding of human nature. As he traveled the roads of Germany by day, he thought of what he would write at night. As he dealt with the daily crises that an empire was experiencing in the courts and assemblies of central Europe, he fused the knowledge of the past with the experience of the present. If we are to believe what Saavedra wrote in the prologue to the reader, *The Royal Politician* was neither conceived nor written in the tranquility of a study or a library. The prologue too has an emblem which is based on Horace (*The Art of Poetry*, 143): "Ex Fumo in Lucem" ("After Smoke, the Light"). Saavedra begins with these words: "During the laborious leisure of my continual journeys through Germany and other countires, I thought about the hundred essays which make up *The Royal Politician*. On stopping at inns for the night, I would write up what I had turned over in my mind along the road, whenever my regular correspondence with the King and his ministers and my other official duties gave me the time to do so" (I, 7).

One of the most terrifying passages in the book is a description of the horrors that were visited on Europe during the years that Saavedra's diplomatic assignment carried him on journeys over its roads. The graphic emblem for Essay XII is almost an inversion of Goya's *Capricho* (*Caprice*) 43, "El sueño de la razón produce monstruos" ("When reason sleeps, monsters are engendered"). Saavedra's graphic shows the sun dispersing nocturnal creatures, and the emblem reads "Excaecat Candor" ("Light Blinds"), for the brilliance of the sun puts to flight the beasts of darkness. The picture he draws is like the dark night of the human soul:

Did tyrants ever devise torments more cruel than those we have seen employed to torture not innocent barbarians but rather the people of cultured, religious, civilized nations? And these cruelties have been employed not against enemies but against the tormenters' own countrymen at a time when the natural order of kinship has been turned topsy-turvy and love of country has been forgotten. Friendly arms have been turned against the very people who paid for them. Their effect has been bloodier than the action of the foe. People could not distinguish between friendly forces and the enemy, between friendship and hostility. Flame and fury have spared no great building, no sacred spot. In a short space of time villages and cities have been reduced to ashes, and towns have been turned into deserts.

The thirst for human blood has been insatiable. Even after the fury of Mars has passed, pistols and swords have been tested on human breasts as if they were the trunks of trees. Eyes have taken pleasure in the contorted visages of death. The chests and bellies of human beings, sliced open, have served as mangers; at times, in the bellies of pregnant women, horses have eaten mixed up in their hay, the tiny half-formed limbs of fetuses.

At the cost of a life, tests have been made to determine how much water a human body contains, or the length of time that it takes to starve a man to death. Virgins dedicated to God have been ravished, girls have been violated in front of their fathers, and married women have been raped before the eyes of their husbands. Women have been sold or bartered in exchange for cows and horses, like booty and spoils, for indecent purposes.

Peasants have been harnessed to pull carts. In order to force them to reveal where they have hidden their valuables, they have been hung by their feet or even by their private parts, and they have been shoved into heated ovens. Before their eyes their babes have been ripped to pieces in order that natural affection for those creatures of their loins might achieve what torture to themselves could not. In forests and woods, where wild beasts take refuge, men could not find safety, because bloodhounds tracked them down. Lakes were not secure from avarice which made ingenious use of hooks and nets to search out treasures hidden in their depths. Even the bones of the dead were disturbed in their resting places as pillagers toppled urns or raised tombstones to seize what was hidden in them. No magic art or diabolical trick went unused in the search for gold and silver (*Idea*, I, 122 - 25).

Saavedra could have been thinking of a hundred campaigns or any of thousands of incidents, but three events from the reality of the times seem to be reflected in these pages of *The Royal Politi-*

cian. In 1625 Christian IV of Denmark invaded the Empire. The Count of Tilly, commander of the field forces of the Catholic League, was aided by that extraordinary adventurer Wallenstein, who secured permission from Ferdinand II to raise an independent army. His promises of high pay and freedom to plunder attracted a motley force of Italians, Swiss, Spaniards, Germans, Poles, Scots, and Englishmen. Wallenstein welcomed Protestant and Catholic alike—as did, by the way, the alliance of the Dutch and the French. His soldiers' loyalty was to him. The army was an unusually effective fighting force, but the plunder and rape of town and countryside by soldiers and camp followers was frightfully destructive. In May of 1631 Tilly captured the Lutheran city of Magdeburg. The garrison was massacred. Citizens were assassinated in the streets, in their homes, even in the churches; and the commander made no move to halt the slaughter. Perhaps twenty thousand people perished. Plundering and fire accompanied the killing. The reaction among the Protestants was of furious indignation. Vengeance was bound to come.

José María Jover, in his book *1635: Historia de una polémica y semblanza de una generación (1635: History of a Polemic and Portrait of a Generation)*, points out that the history of the Thirty Years' War was written by the victors, that is, by the French and the Protestants. The atrocities of Wallenstein's forces and the sack of Magdeburg loom large in their history books. The accounts of another great holocaust have been systematically excluded. The Dutch and the French seized the undefended town of Tirlemont (Tienen) in Brabant province of the Spanish Netherlands in 1635 and vented their pent-up wrath on the inhabitants. Cornelis Jansen, later the famed Bishop of Ypres, was nearby at Louvain, and he left us in his *Mars Gallicus (Gallic Mars; 1635)* a moving account of this disaster. The attackers burned the hospital with the patients still in it. They put soldiers and civilians alike to torment by fire. They tore infants from their mothers' breasts, dashed some against walls, stabbed others, and threw still others into the flames. They murdered monks, nuns, priests. They profaned holy vessels and fed the Sacrament to their horses.[11] The fury spilled over into other towns in the area, and Jansen continues his account by relating the Dantesque horrors which the French and Dutch armies, with refined savagery, visited upon the inhabitants.

Even people today, inured to total war, civilian bombing, concentration camps, and all the horrors of the twentieth century, must find repugnant those accounts of brutal inhumanity. In his play

Mother Courage and Her Children (written 1939; performed 1941), a twentieth-century dramatist, Bertolt Brecht, has vividly portrayed the life of Europe's common people during the bloody conflicts of the Thirty Years' War. His character, Anna Fierling, nicknamed "Mother Courage," follows either the Swedish or the imperial armies as an itinerant trader. She lives by the war, selling the soldiers shoes, shirts, brandy, and other items from her covered wagon. She must pay the price of war. One by one her three children—each by a different father—are shot. Mother Courage, determined to continue trading, wearily pulls her cart to overtake the army.[12]

In our private world of the imagination, where reality and fancy meet, we can wonder whether Mother Courage with her cart, travelling along a German road, ever crossed the path of the diplomat Saavedra Fajardo as he rode in his carriage and meditated on the essay he would put to paper that night.

VI *The Backing of Authority*

However much Saavedra Fajardo may have valued nature and experience as the basis of wisdom, he yet found in books his principal sources. Like *Republic of Letters, The Royal Politician* is replete with erudition, which is documented in marginal notes. However, it need not be concluded that Saavedra's reading was as vast as the notes would make it seem. His citations are often those that he could read in other authors. In the case of the Bible, however, of which there are some five hundred citations, the precision is as worthy of note as the abundance.[13] We may justifiably surmise that it was a volume that accompanied the tonsured abbé on his journeys. The books of the Bible to which he refers most frequently are Ecclesiastes, Proverbs, and Psalms.

Classical authors appear in great numbers. Of them, Aristotle and Tacitus particularly stand out. The *Politics* of course loomed large in a book such as *The Royal Politician*. For Tacitus, the severe Roman historian, Saavedra shows a remarkable predilection. There are almost seven hundred citations from him. Saavedra was not alone in his admiration. In seventeenth-century Spain was a whole school of Tacitists. Spanish writers may have felt kinship for the severe moralist who bent his principles in the attempt to stave off the disasters of a declining empire. Juan de Mariana, in *The King and His Education,* commends Tacitus to the prince saying: "Reading him will permit seeing, as in a mirror, a representation of our own times in the perils and misfortunes of others."[14] The Tacitists in Spain are associated with the Machiavellians, and

Saavedra himself, despite the predilection he showed, recognized the evil doctrines implicit in Tacitus. In *Republic of Letters* he observes that Tacitus remained unknown until a certain Fleming introduced him to the modern world, and he comments: "I don't know but that he may have done more harm to the public weal than the inventor of gunpowder, such are the tryannical doctrines and poison that have been drawn from this source. Guillaume Budé said of him that he was among the most wicked of writers."[15]

Among medieval authors, Saavedra is indebted in a general way to St. Thomas, especially to his *De Legibus (Concerning Laws)*. More apparent in his citations is his debt to the *Siete Partidas (Seven Parts)*, the compilation of laws made for Alfonso X the Wise. Although in *Republic of Letters* Saavedra professed disdain for the monarch who let his crown slip from his head while he gazed at the stars (pp. 146 - 47), and criticized him in the essay "Either Rise or Fall," he nevertheless cites him some sixty times in *The Royal Politician*.

Among contemporary writers, Juan de Mariana, especially in his *History of Spain*, furnished Saavedra with historical incidents from which to draw moral or political lessons. To be sure, though Saavedra praised Mariana's intelligence, he criticized him in *Republic of Letters*—who did not come in for knocks in that little volume?—and again in *Gothic Crown*, for being unfair to Spain: "In order to gain a reputation among foreign nations for being truthful and dispassionate, he does not forgive his own country and even condemns it on doubtful issues" (p. 125).

Saavedra owed a great debt to other writers of emblems, as his own annotations to *The Royal Politician* clearly show. The whole repertoire of sixteenth- and seventeenth-century emblem writers, both Spanish and foreign, is to be found: Sebastián de Covarrubias, Juan de Solórzano, Hernando de Soto, Pérez de Herrera, Alciati, Schoonhovius, Junius Hadrianus, Boissardus, Antoine de Bourgogne, Brissard, Camerario, Buxhorn, and especially Jacob Bruck, called Angermunt, whose emblems, like Saavedra's, were political as well as moral. In some cases the emblems may coincide because of a similarity of subject matter; in others the coincidence may be simply the memory of his readings; but in the case of certain unusual symbols, direct adaption is evident.[16]

Cervantes in the prologue to Part I of the *Quixote* makes fun of authors who load themselves down with erudition. He is loath, he says, to imagine what the public will think of his tale, "wholly lacking in learning and wisdom, without marginal citations or notes at the end of the book when other works of this sort, even though they be fabulous and profane, are so packed with maxims from Aristotle and Plato and the whole crowd of philosophers as to fill the reader with admiration and lead him to regard the author as a well-read, learned, and eloquent individual" (I, Prologue, p. 12).

The trend was medieval, but beginning with the Marquis of Santillana, writers overdid documentation more and more until they reached the point where they could say nothing without giving a classical source. However, Saavedra Fajardo felt he had to defend his abundant use of erudition. In his prologue he informs the reader: "If I mix erudition into my essays, it is not to show off my knowledge but to sharpen the wit of the prince and to make learning easy" (I, 68). His erudition, then, was supposed to have pedagogical value, but in fact he could not escape the fashion which was partly display and partly the desire for authoritative backing.

VII   *The Christian Virtue of Prudence*

Two themes run through every essay of *The Royal Politician:* the Christian virtues and the mortal sins. The four cardinal virtues—prudence, justice, fortitude, and temperance—ought to be magnified in the monarch. Each has a significant role in the moral conduct of the ordinary Christian; in the character and acts of the monarch, each assumes an added political significance. The greatest of the virtues is of course prudence. Princes, like ordinary men, possess mental faculties which permit them to act. These faculties are reason, understanding, and will. Man's reason, which distinguished him from the beasts, works on the materials supplied by sensation, the fantasy, and the memory, and enables him to act with judgment. His understanding operates upward toward the immaterial world. It relates man to the angels, who, as the sixteenth-century psychologist Huarte de San Juan said, possessed it to an extraordinary degree in order that they might approach nearer to God.[17] Baltasar Gracián, a younger contemporary of Saavedra, believed that the understanding was a gift granted man by heaven and that, unless a man possessed it, he could not achieve greatness.[18] The will, finally, is the executive faculty of the soul; it acts on the basis of the reason and understanding. Interpreted as free will, it enables a man to choose between good and evil.

Each of man's faculties—the senses, the fantasy, memory, reason, understanding, will—possesses elements which may lead man to degradation if he makes the wrong choices; but another aspect of each faculty aids him in the realization of his higher self. The sum of these good elements, when possessed in a high degree, endows him with the supreme virtue of prudence, which is primarily Christian but also political. In the moral and political literature of the sixteenth century references to this quality are frequent. The word appears, for example, on almost every page of Machiavelli's *The Prince*. It is a recurring concept in Saavedra's *The Royal Politician*. Between the ideas of the two writers on this subject there are points of agreement as well as sharp differences.

Prudence, as a Christian virtue, governs man's relations with God and serves as his guide in the exercise of his faculties and the other cardinal virtues. Juan de Mariana stated its function thus: "Prudence is the power of the mind that looks ahead into every aspect, remembering the past, appraising the present, divining the future, surmising secrets from what is manifested. . . . Without [it] the remainder of life would necessarily lie in the gloom and mud."[19] Saavedra Fajardo makes a similar statement in Essay II, "Ad Omnia ("Toward All Things"), as he discusses what we could call, in the cant of today, "early childhood education" *(Idea,* I, 32). The lexicographer Covarrubias described the prudent person as "the wise, self-controlled man who weighs all problems with great understanding."[20] The significance of prudence in the exercise of free will is clearly established by the lexicographers who composed the definition of prudence for the eighteenth-century *Diccionario de Autoridades (Dictionary of Authorities):* "it teaches man to distinguish between good and evil, in order to follow the former and avoid the latter."[21]

The moral and political writers of the period use other terms in connection with prudence, and these must be distinguished from it. The principal ones are discretion *(discreción)*, sharpness, *(agudeza)*, astuteness *(astucia)*, and wit *(ingenio)*. The nearest of these to prudence is discretion, but there is a clear difference, as Margaret Bates has shown in her study of the use of "discretion" and related words in the works of Cervantes.[22] The distinction is to be found in the fact that prudence is a virtue and consequently leads only to a good end. Discretion may lead to either a good or a bad end. Hence, discretion figures largely in novels and plays while prudence is emphasized in didactic literature. Discretion was thought to have its seat in the understanding whence it directed the will and man's lower faculties. It included foresight, a certain wariness, courtesy, a sense of values. Associated with it were wisdom and wit. Like prudence, its primary source is God. It may also be acquired at court, or from education and travel, or through experience, age, noble birth, and love. The deciding distinction, however, lies in the fact that prudence is a cardinal virtue while discretion is not.

Sharpness and astuteness, of course, are further removed from prudence, but they figure conspicuously in the works of writers touched with Tacitism and Machiavellianism. Hence, Saavedra, though fascinated, still stands at arm's length from them, while Gracián sometimes embraces them. One of the latter's books is entitled *Agudeza y arte de ingenio (Sharpness and Art of Wit).* Sharpness denotes subtleness, inventiveness, originality. Compared with discretion, however, it is inconstant.

Astuteness is farther removed from the element of good, but in writers affected by Tacitism and Machiavellianism it even becomes identified with prudence. Saavedra himself wrote: "Sometimes it is advisable to clothe force with astuteness and indignation with benignity, dissimulating and accommodating oneself to the moment and to the people" *(Idea,* II, 166). Thus dissimulation and accommodation become elements in the political concept of prudence. The association of prudence and astuteness received impetus in one of the most popular figures of the period, the simile of the fox and the lion which Machiavelli had used in *The Prince:* "A prince . . . must imitate the fox and the lion, for the lion cannot protect himself from traps, and the fox cannot defend himself from wolves. He must therefore be a fox to defend himself from traps, and a lion to frighten wolves. Those princes that wish to be only lions do not understand this. Therefore, a prudent ruler ought not to keep faith when by so doing it would be against his interest, and when the reasons which make him bind himself no longer exist."[23] A stern moralist like Pedro de Rivadeneira rejected this concept of prudence: "Prudence should be real and not feigned, Christian not political, a solid virtue and not deceitful astuteness."[24] This is the position that Saavedra also takes after some irresolution.

"Wit" is probably the best translation for *ingenio,* but in the seventeenth century the word did service for "intelligence" as well. We may think of it as meaning intelligence plus subtlety, and as not far removed from *agudeza.* In a letter from Regensburg in 1637 on the state of Europe, Saavedra used *ingenio* in the sense of "intelligence" rather than "wit": "Matters have reached such an extreme that we cannot count on force alone but must use intelligence to resolve our problems. . . ."[25]

The virtue of prudence, in the concept of Spanish moralists of a political persuasion, was composed of several parts, among them moderation, knowledge of self, accommodation, dissimulation, and distrust. Moderation—associated naturally with that other Christian virtue, temperance—meant the Aristotelian golden mean and had been the subject of praise by Christian writers for centuries. The virtuous man should avoid extremes, and the good ruler should do likewise. "The art of government," wrote Saavedra, "lies in shunning extremes, while seeking the middle road, where the virtues dwell" *(Idea,* II, 146). Prudent moderation counsels the prince whether to speak much or little, whether to appear in public often or seldom *(Idea,* I, 176; II, 136). It suggests to him how to grant favors and how to mete out punishment, because extreme liberality and excessive rigor are both imprudent *(Idea,* I, 236; II, 146 - 47). Most important of all, it teaches the prince to control his passions so that he acts in accordance with reason *(Idea,* II, 148). Saavedra chooses from the book of nature an example of moderation: Nature has placed between the rigors of summer and winter the benignity of spring and autumn *(Idea,* IV, 37 - 38).

Knowledge of oneself was a paramount part of prudence: "Know thyself." Plutarch ascribed the admonition to Plato and said it was inscribed upon the Delphic oracle; and it was attributed to several other classical writers. St. Paul gave the same counsel to Christians. The task was peculiar to men, for the angels already knew themselves; and beasts could not, for they were not endowed with reason. Such introspection, far from being immodest, was a necessary task if man was not to resemble the beasts. Through a knowledge of himself, Saavedra says, man can follow the path of moderation, for only by knowing his passions, his inclinations, the way he reacts to the outside world, his defects and his weaknesses as well as his good qualities, can he learn to control himself *(Idea,* II, 152). In the modern world, which has divorced itself from Christian principle, we say that a man is seeking his identity; if he does not find it, he suffers an identity crisis.

While knowledge of oneself is important, it is equally essential to know others, for that is the basis of accommodation, which in turn is an essential element of prudence. The doctrine of accommodation goes beyond adjusting oneself to other people; it includes accommodation to time, place, and circumstances. A man, and especially a prince, must be able to change in accordance with specific conditions. "Government cannot be as rigorous as it ought to be but rather as firm as it is possible for it to be," wrote Saavedra. "Even the rule of God accommodates itself to human weakness" *(Idea,* II, 154). Hence the prince must understand the nature of the men with whom he deals, whether they be his own subjects or his enemies.

He will take into account the circumstances of the moment and be governed by its particulars. He will not undertake more than he can accomplish *(Idea, II, 66). St. Thomas advised the ruler that a sense of accommodation would teach the prince to choose the lesser of two evils.[26] Saavedra follows him in Essay XXXVII, "Minimum Eligendum" ("Choosing the Lesser"), which is heavily influenced also by Tacitus.

From accommodation to dissimulation is but a short step. In his dialogue on ideal courtly life, Baldassare Castiglione had sanctioned it for the courtier in lesser matters. When we find that so stern a moralist as Rivadeneira also counsels it, we recognize that it has become a part of the Christian picture. Dissimulation, it can be said, is the prudent Christian's accommodation to Machiavellianism. To a discussion of dissimulation Saavedra Fajardo devotes Essay XLIII, entitled "Ut Sciat Regnare" ("In Order to Reign"). The conclusion of the complete Latin phrase is "sciat dissimulare" so that the message is "He who would learn to reign must know how to dissimulate." Throughout his work Saavedra applies the doctrine of dissimulation to specific cases. He advises that on occasions of danger it is prudent, perhaps even courageous, to dissimulate rather than attack openly *(Idea, II, 95). Dissimulation in war, he says, is permissible: "It is legitimate to deceive the enemy whom it is licit to kill" *(Idea, IV, 21).

But Spanish moralists struggled with the problem, trying to set limits, especially in the fields of diplomacy and internal politics. In the essay "In Order to Reign" Saavedra made a noble attempt to distinguish between real deceit and licit dissimulation:

Dissimulation and astuteness can be considered licit when they neither deceive the opponent nor bring discredit to the prince. In such cases, I do not judge them to be vices, but rather prudence, or virtues born of it, which are convenient and necessary in the person who would govern. This situation occurs when the prudent man, aware that self-preservation is at stake, has recourse to astuteness to conceal matters in accordance with the circumstances of time, place, and people, while also observing a consistency between heart and tongue, between thought and words. One should avoid that dissimulation which lies about concrete facts with deceitful ends, or which aims to make one's opponent understand what is not so. But that dissimulation is legitimate which keeps him from understanding what is so. Thus it is proper to use neutral or ambiguous words, or to say one thing instead of another giving a different meaning to the subject, not with the intent to deceive, but in order to take precautions or forestall deception, or for other legitimate ends *(Idea, II, 167).

Saavedra has here sketched the type of dissimulation most common-
ly approved: to speak in such a way that the other person mis-
understands or does not understand even though what one actually
says is not deceitful. The good Fray Luis de Granada had lent an
aura of approbation to such dissimulation: "It is prudent . . . to
be able to control one's tongue, . . . knowing well what may be
said and what ought to be kept secret, knowing when to speak and
when to be silent."[27]

Gracián moved the line between licit and illicit dissimulation
toward the sinister side. He made dissimulation an instrument for
the preservation of a reputation, a subject of great concern to men
in seventeenth-century Spain. His reasoning is logical. Defects mar
the good name of the prince; if he has any, therefore, they must be
concealed. Dissimulation, which might better be called conceal-
ment or deceit or feigning, is the instrument.[28]

Gracián verged close upon Machiavellianism. In the same
Chapter XVIII of the *The Prince* in which Machiavelli drew the
parallel of the fox and the lion is a paragraph which created a
veritable fury among stern Spanish moralists. Having discussed
those admirable qualities that are desirable in a prince, Machiavelli
writes: "It is not . . . necessary for a prince to have all the above-
named qualities, but it is very necessary to seem to have them. I
would even be bold to say that to possess them and always to
observe them is dangerous, but to appear to possess them is useful.
Thus it is well to seem merciful, faithful, humane, sincere, religious,
and also to be so; but you must have the mind so disposed that
when it is needful to be otherwise you may be able to change to the
opposite qualities."[29] Spanish moralists could not countenance this.
Even Gracián, in more lucid moments, recognized that virtues
should be real and not feigned: "The hero must truly possess every
gift and every excellent quality but feign none. Pretense is the ruin
of greatness."[30]

Saavedra, like Gracián, like Machiavelli, perceived the usefulness
of dissimulation. He tried to incorporate the concept into his Christian view, and hence he made his distinctions: Dissimulation must
not become deceit (*Idea*, II, 167). It must not preclude the ability to
act in good faith (*Idea*, II, 172 - 73). And, most importantly, it must
not be applied to religion (*Idea*, II, 3). Dissimulation, of course,
works two ways. A prince may practice it, but he may also be the
victim of it. Hence an important part of prudence is distrust.
Saavedra puts the problem thus: "Self-preservation obliges us to be
distrustful. If we are not, we lack foresight, and all is endangered.

The prince who places his trust in very few people will govern his state better. The only sure way to be self-reliant is not to subject oneself to the will or the decision of another; for, who can put his trust in the human heart which is hidden deep in the breast? The tongue conceals and dissembles its intentions, and the eyes and the movement of the body contradict its designs" *(Idea,* II, 273). But distrust may be carried too far. Moderation will teach the prince to strike a happy medium between credulity and excessive doubt: "Let the prince be trusting and believe in others, but let him be alert to the fact that he may be deceived" *(Idea,* II, 275).

VIII   *The Virtues of Justice, Fortitude, and Temperance*

Prudence was, in the concept of seventeenth-century moralists, the supreme virtue for both the private person and the prince. The other cardinal virtues—justice, fortitude, and temperance—were, however, especially significant for the character of the ruler. Of these, a sense of justice was fundamental. Scholastic doctrine had distinguished three types of justice: legal justice, commercial justice, and justice in distribution. Rivadeneira emphasized the last in a simple definition which he intends to be a general one: "The virtue of justice . . . gives equally to each man what is rightfully his."[31]

Saavedra Fajardo, who had taken his degree in canonical law at Salamanca, shows most interest in legal justice, especially in its practical aspects. He is, for example, concerned about the multiplicity of laws. Like Don Quixote in his advice to Sancho on the government of the island of Barataria, Saavedra speaks out for moderation in the number of laws: "When there are a great many laws, they cause confusion and are forgotten; and if they cannot be observed, they are despised" *(Idea,* I, 262). He deplores the abundance of legal disputes and their unnecessary prolixity. He praises Isabel the Catholic for the dispatch with which she once liquidated a great number of cases that were pending in Sevilla. Bringing in the experience of his European travel, he lauds the Swiss for their speedy justice: "The litigant is better off to lose a case that is quickly decided than to win it after years of litigation" *(Idea,* I, 267).

An important aspect of justice is clemency. In the execution of justice the prince may be required to act harshly, but the ideal is clemency. When, in the reign of Philip II, historians undertook the rehabilitation of the fourteenth-century monarch Pedro the Cruel, they renamed him Pedro the Just. Christian clemency, the moralists point out, approximates man to God. On the practical side, the political writer notes, undue rigor may cause the prince to lose his kingdom if he provokes his subjects to rebellion.

Fortitude is of special importance in the character of the prince, for it is both a Christian virtue and an indispensable political qualification. Machiavelli's ideas on fortitude seemed singularly iniquitous to Spanish moralists. In the *Discourses* the Florentine advanced the theory that the pagans were more energetic and ferocious in their actions because they esteemed more the things of this world. Christianity had had, he believed, a softening effect on men because it placed emphasis on the rewards of the next world.[32] Rivadeneira refuted Machiavelli in a chapter in which he recites the names and deeds of valorous Christian warriors.[33] Saavedra associates moral fortitude with physical courage and values the joint exercise of prudence and fortitude. Prudence points the proper method in matters involving the use of strength; fortitude enables the prince to execute resolutely and bravely his determination (*Idea*, II, 150 - 51).

The practical implications of the virtue of fortitude attracted Saavedra. A monarchy, he observes, is built on strength and courage, but it can be lost if indulgence in delights brings weakness (*Idea*, III, 117). Subjects despise a king who indulges in debilitating pleasures; they think him weak and incapable of defending them (*Idea*, III, 111). To be sure, the king should not undertake needless conquests, which will lead to injustice, tyranny, and weakness. Within his kingdom, however, he must cultivate the military arts. To the outside world he must present a bold front. In particular, he should stress the art of diplomacy. This is a point of view characteristic both of Saavedra himself and of the period in which he lived. The result of the emphasis on fortitude was the advocacy of preparedness for war, which Saavedra associates with the preservation of peace. Neglect of armament, he says, will be interpreted as weakness: "A country that is unprepared attracts enemies and brings war upon itself" (*Idea*, IV, 195). Peace is the aim, but the objective must be backed by power: "Among mankind there can be no peace if respect for force does not repress men's ambitions" (*Idea*, IV, 195).

The maintenance of a good army necessarily concerned those who considered the practical side of fortitude. In the sixteenth century Spain's famed infantry regiments (called *tercios*, "thirds," because each was divided into three classes according to their weapons: lances, harquebuses, and muskets) were the pride of the nation and the fear of Europe. So they remained until·the crushing defeat of Rocroi in 1643—three years after the publication of *The Royal Politician*. In the early years of the seventeenth century Suárez de Figueroa could still say of Spanish soldiers: "Who does not respect them? The Turk fears them. Prester John loves them. The Persian admires them; and every potentate wants them for his friends."[34] Political writers stress the need for the maintenance of discipline, for its weakening during the Thirty Years' War was leading to the decline and the eventual defeat of the army. Discipline cannot be maintained, however, it is frequently pointed out, if just rewards are not forthcoming. There is a special interest in promotion on the basis of merit. Saavedra is cautious on this point. He realizes that inherited nobility and courage do not always go together so that the prince should reward merit wherever he finds it. On the other hand, particularly in times of peace, important positions should not be entrusted to men of low birth (*Idea*, I, 223).

The last of the cardinal virtues, temperance, evoked somewhat less interest in the political writers than did prudence, justice, and fortitude. Its importance was not overlooked, however. The application of the principles of temperance to the life of the court produced much criticism of extravagance. Saavedra censures the enormous expenditures made on dress, jewelry, banquets, festivals, and pastimes. These indulgences on the part of the king (the Count-Duke of Olivares encouraged Philip IV in his lavish tastes) cause his subjects to imitate him so that the whole monarchy is corrupted by vice and impoverished by extravagance.

The narrow line that existed between virtue and vice is illustrated by some aspects of temperance. Moderation is the determinant. In the middle, for example, is liberality, but on one side lies prodigality and on the other avarice, a deadly sin. Saavedra believed that liberality, or generosity, or largesse, were qualities especially to be admired in the prince (*Idea*, II, 137 - 38). Liberality was a delicate matter, for it was linked to the touchy subject of honor and the distribution of rewards, and the wrong decisions could lead to trouble (*Idea*, III, 65 - 67). If the deviation was toward avarice, the prince was in deeper trouble. "Cupidity in princes destroys their states" (*Idea*, III, 11); and it is equally pernicious in his ministers and subjects: "Where avarice reigns, peace and tranquility are lacking. The nation is engulfed in the turmoil of quarrels, sedition, and civil war" (*Idea*, III, 10).

IX   The Mortal Sins

In the king's quarters in the Royal Monastery of San Lorenzo del Escorial there was, in Saavedra's time, a table on the top of which were depicted scenes representative of the Seven Deadly Sins. The pictures had been done by the Dutch painter Hieronymus Bosch (1450? - 1516), who lived in the period of the Catholic Sovereigns. The table must have come to Spain during the time of the Infanta Juana's marriage to Philip the Handsome of Flanders or in the reign of their son Charles, who became Emperor Charles V. On his visits to the Escorial, Philip IV, Saavedra's king, was reminded of how a man or a monarch could endanger his immortal soul. Today, the table stands in Madrid's Prado Museum where a visitor may count the ways a human being can sin. In the center of the rectangular top is a picture of the sorrowing Christ with the Latin warning, "Cave, cave, Dominus videt" ("Take care, for God is watching"). In a circle surrounding Him are painted seven scenes each devoted to one of the deadly sins, which, unforgiven, condemn a man to an eternity of expiation: pride, envy, wrath, lust, sloth, avarice, and gluttony. In a circle in each of the four corners are scenes representing the last stages of man: death, judgment, hell, and heaven.

Reminders of man's depraved nature are ever present in Baroque art and literature. The Christian virtues and the deadly sins are the warp and the woof of the backdrop against which Baroque man plays out the drama of his life. The denouement is death and judgment. To some vices Saavedra gave special attention. Envy has been said to be a peculiarly Iberian vice, but if we are to judge from the attention given to it by European writers of emblems, it was endemic to the whole continent, as it is, indeed, in human nature. To it Saavedra devotes Essay IX entitled "Sui Vindex" in earlier editions and "Sibimet Invidia Vindex" in later ones ("Envy Is Its Own Avenger"). The graphic shows two fierce hounds, representing envy, which attack the trophies of Hercules; when they attempt to dig their fangs into his cudgel, their wounded mouths drip blood. Saavedra reminds the reader of a verse from Proverbs (14.30): "Vita carnium, sanitas cordium; putredo ossium invidia" ("A tranquil heart puts flesh on a man; envy rots his bones"). With Tacitus he observes that as the good fortune of one man waxes, the envy of another grows (Idea, IX, 91).

Like many of the essays, this one, though aimed at the education of the prince, is directed to the moral edification of all men. Indeed, in writing on the subject of envy, Saavedra saw himself the victim of the envy of others. "There are many reasons to pity the author of this book and few or none to envy him. Yet there are people who envy his labors and his unremitting hardships, which go unnoticed and unrewarded" *(Idea,* IX, 94). The touch of self-pity ought to be forgiven. Saavedra rarely injects his own personality into his essays; when he does, we detect that he felt deeply about the subject.

Saavedra devotes Essay VIII to the sin of anger and Essay LIII to avarice. But throughout the 101 essays the theme of man's sins is ever present. The prince, a man of the flesh like his subjects, may sin like them; but in him vice is magnified. In "Either Rise or Fall," for example, Saavedra cited the lust of Roderick, the last Gothic king, as a cause for the fall of his monarchy. The sloth of Juan I of Aragon and Juan II of Castile was their undoing. Alfonso X of Castile was avaricious. The recurring theme of the essays is man's struggle against his lower nature, the conflict between his virtues and his vices for the possession of his soul.

X *Style and Content*

The Royal Politician is a book that a reader is likely to dip into rather than read straight through. It is a collection of essays with an underlying theme. Although the slender thread of narration follows a theoretical prince from the cradle to the grave, the inclination of a reader is to choose an essay at a particular point where the graphic or the motto or a striking introductory sentence awakens his interest. His attention is then ensnared by Saavedra's style. Saavedra wrote at a period when Spanish prose style was either afflicted or enhanced, depending on one's point of view, by cultism and conceptism. Cultism, which resembles euphuism in the history of English literature, affected the language when writers sought beautiful, striking effects. The mode of expression tended to exclude the uneducated, the uninitiated, and the literal minded. The result was, in the words of the poet Pedro Soto de Rojas, a "paradise closed to the many, gardens open to the few."[35] Saavedra is not usually cultist. He directed himself to a cultivated reader, to be sure; but he had serious points to communicate, and it behooved him to seek clarity of expression.

Conceptism affected ideas. The conceptist writer sought to express striking, original thoughts, while the cultist writer strove to phrase a trivial idea in an especially inventive way. Conceptist writers were wits, and the best of them—Quevedo and Gracián, for example—were men of true genius. To be sure, cultism and conceptism were not rigorously separate, and they were sometimes to be found affecting a single writer. However, Quevedo himself specifically rejected many of the cultist modes. Saavedra Fajardo also is to be associated more closely with the conceptist group. Nonetheless, because he felt the pressing need to impart his moral precepts to a wide public, he did not depart very far from the standard means of communication.

Saavedra uses figurative language as the Bible does. He employs aphoristic expression as Tacitus does. Such were his sources and such was the language with which his readers were familiar. Compared with either Quevedo or Gracián, Saavedra uses language and expressions that are relatively more straightforward, relatively less adorned. A modern critic has observed that Saavedra has frequent recourse to an anecdote, an historical reference, or a human event. Such concrete illustrations illuminate the abstraction and have a clarifying effect on the style itself.[36]

The purity of the style commended *The Royal Politician* to generations of Spaniards. When Baroque thought became so convoluted that there was no way of following it, Spanish writers turned to Saavedra as a model of prose style. Writing in 1725, the scholar Gregorio Mayáns y Siscar acknowledged his debt to Saavedra Fajardo in these words: "The master from whom I have learned to appreciate the purity and expressiveness of the Castilian tongue has been and is Don Diego Saavedra Farjardo. . . . To the frequent perusal of his highly polished writings I owe my own command of style such as it is. . . ."[37] Mayáns proposes Saavedra as a model for those who wish to avoid the "false adornment and useless verbosity" of that late Baroque eloquence which still prevailed in his day. Mayáns, who showed himself to be tainted by Baroque taste, continues eloquently: "Some people like a style which, like a false gem, glistens with superficial brilliance. Others, with better reason, prefer an unpretentious style which, like the rugged oyster shell, encloses great worth in its hidden depths. The sensible judge of styles prefers one which, like the priceless diamond, possesses great depths and is also artfully polished with elegant skill" (p. xii). The essayist Benito Jerónimo Feijoo took exception to one point that Mayáns made about Saavedra's style. Mayáns thought it a virtue that the author of *The Royal Politician* never employed colloquialisms such as Quevedo was wont to use in some of his works. Feijoo agreed that Saavedra's style was elegant, but he thought it would have been invigorated had he aptly employed some colloquial expressions.[38]

The Royal Spanish Academy was created in 1713 and began compiling its great dictionary based on authoritative writers. Saavedra Fajardo was selected as one of those authorities, and three of his works—*Republic of Letters, The Royal Politician,* and *Gothic Crown*—supplied examples on which definitions were based. The six volumes of the familiarly known *Dictionary of Authorities* appeared between 1726 and 1739, less than a century after Saavedra was writing. Of some two hundred authorities, however, Saavedra is often singled out with a few others as a writer of special distinction. Thus, in Cadalso's *Cartas marruecas (Moroccan Letters),* the character Nuño Núñez—Cadalso's alter ego—thinks of the names of five authorities on word meaning, naming them in this order: Antonio de Solís, Saavedra, Cervantes, Juan de Mena, and Alfonso X the Wise.[39]

Saavedra Fajardo's reputation survived into the Neoclassic period. At the end of the eighteenth century José Luis Munárriz prepared a Spanish version of the *Lectures on Rhetoric* (1783) which Hugh Blair had delivered as professor at Edinburgh University. In *Lecciones sobre la retórica y las bellas artes (Lessons on Rhetoric and the Fine Arts;* 1798 - 1801) Munárriz substituted Spanish examples for many of the references to English literature that Blair used. For the purposes of a detailed stylistic analysis, Blair had examples by Joseph Addison and Jonathan Swift. Munárriz substituted Cervantes for Lesson XX and Saavedra Fajardo for Lesson XXI. The example by Cervantes was from *Don Quixote* (Part II, Ch. XVIII), "What Happened to Don Quixote in the Castle or Home of the Gentleman with the Green Greatcoat. . . ." Munárriz, like his fellow Neoclassics, admired Cervantes's style. Also, like them, he refused to admit perfection where it did not exist. "Without question the ease and freedom with which Cervantes handled his language caused him to commit oversights which other writers with more care and circumspection would have avoided, although their genius was not comparable to his."[40] Munárriz then proceeded with a detailed criticism of the chapter from the *Quixote.*

Munárriz is equally severe in his consideration of Saavedra Fajardo. Comparing the two writers, he comments: "Cervantes's style is periodic and diffuse; Saavedra's is abrupt. In Cervantes one finds redundancy and carelessness; in Saavedra, a lack of unity and order. Cervantes's work is a novel, and its style corresponds to that of a narrative. Saavedra's work which I analyze is a treatise, and its style is didactic and instructive" (II, 265). Because of the "unfortunate period" in which Saavedra was educated, his style was "contaminated," according to Munárriz. The critic finds Saavedra at times cultist, but he is more frequently conceptist. He is however, serious and austere, and he never fails to observe purity of diction. "His *Political Essays* are probably the most useful and pithy work that the Castilian language possesses. In his time there was no other writer capable of transmitting to posterity with equal ease maxims that are so fertile in truths of the first importance" (II, 266).

Having demonstrated his respect for Saavedra, the critic then begins to rip apart his prose style. Munárriz chose Essay VI, "Politioribus Ornantur Litterae" ("Letters Are an Adornment to Political Men"). After quoting the long first sentence, Munárriz observes that an introduction ought to be clear, precise, and simple. Saavedra intemperately displays his erudition and, far from clarifying his thought, makes it confusing. Continuing through the essay sentence by sentence, Munárriz praises Saavedra for a well-sustained metaphor and for an aptly chosen adjective. He chides him for failure to repeat the definite article when he should have, and for the improper use of the causal *pues* (since). He congratulates him on the simplicity of a narrative paragraph that supports his argument, but reprehends him subsequently when he forgets the argument he has just made to sustain an opposite point of view. "This intellectual inconsistency is the result of not having thought through the matter sufficiently well, because lack of meditation always has the effect of making language and style confusing and equivocal" (II, 276).

By the time Munárriz has finished with his analysis of Saavedra's essay, he has convinced us that we are reading a hastily conceived and poorly written piece by a schoolboy rather than the serious work of one of the great prose stylists of Spain's Golden Age. Munárriz recognizes in himself the penchant of the rhetorician to belittle and warns his reader: "We may have writers completely free of the defects I have observed in [both Cervantes and Saavedra Fajardo], but they generally do not have half the merit of these two" (II, 290).

Young Romantics rejected Saavedra Fajardo. In Mesonero Romanos's *costumbrista* article "El romanticismo y los románticos" ("Romanticism and Romantics"), the author tells us that his fictional nephew, who Gallicized Spanish, also repudiated Cervantes, Quevedo, Saavedra, and Moratín, in favor of the latest French writers: Hugo, Dumas, Balzac, and Sand.[41] Thus, it is not surprising that in the years after the 1819 edition of selected works, Saavedra's books were not published during the Romantic period. However, the Biblioteca de Autores Españoles itself is one of the great achievements of the mature Romantics, and in 1853, with Volume 25, Saavedra's works were again in print. Saavedra Fajardo occupied a distinguished place in Spanish letters in the esteem of the authors of the Generation of 1898, for they appreciated good style and clear thinking on subjects of universal concern. The greatest stylist of the generation, Azorín, was especially devoted to Saavedra and founded a society which he called the Friends of Saavedra Fajardo.[42]

CHAPTER 4

The Folly of Europe

IN early July, 1640, Saavedra Fajardo traveled from Munich to Vienna. There, on the tenth of that month, he signed the dedication of *The Royal Politician* to Prince Baltasar Carlos. He had gone to the court of the Austrian Hapsburgs to consult with diplomatic colleagues concerning the Spanish posture in the forthcoming Diet of councillors of the Holy Roman Empire. It was to be held in Regensburg, also known by its medieval name of Ratisbona. The city was situated in the Upper Palatinate on the Danube at the river's northernmost bend and at a distance of eighty-five miles from Munich. Delegates from all the states of the Empire, both Catholic and Protestant, which had the right to send electors, took part in these great formal assemblies.

The Diet opened on September 14, 1640. Don Francisco de Melo, with the title of ambassador extraordinary, was on his way from Vienna to attend as an envoy of Spain. Representing the "house and circle of Burgundy" were Peter Weyms of Luxembourg, Antoine Brun of the Franche-Comté, and Saavedra Fajardo.[1] From Regensburg Saavedra corresponded with Baltasar Rambeck, one of Duke Maximilian's secretaries in Munich, although communications were difficult because the lines were often cut by the enemy's operations. In his letters he urged that Francisco de Melo be given the honors due him as he passed through Munich; he asked that the proofs for *The Royal Politician*, which was being printed in Munich, be sent to him in Regensburg; and he requested that three hundred skins of wine for Melo's use be passed free by customs.[2]

Two problems confronted the Diet. One was the possibility of peace negotiations between the Empire on one side and France and Sweden on the other. The second concerned the organization of the imperial armies, in particular the quartering of soldiers, their maintenance, and their discipline. The Protestant bloc in the Diet opposed all positive measures and used dilatory tactics in an attempt to prevent action. In January, 1641, a Protestant army under the Swedish general Johan Banner attempted to assault the city, crossing the frozen Danube, with the intention of disbanding the Diet and seizing some of the Catholic leaders. Perhaps Saavedra was on their list. By that time, however, *The Royal Politician* was completed. He had corrected the proofs, and the book had appeared in Munich at the end of 1640.

Shortly after the Diet opened, Philip IV made Saavedra a Knight of Santiago. The decree was dated September 18, 1640, subject to proof of pure blood and noble lineage. On September 24 Saavedra's agent in Madrid presented his genealogy to the Council of Military Orders. The receipt was signed by the distinguished author of *Política de Dios y gobierno de Cristo* (*The Politics of God and the Government of Christ*; 1626), Francisco de Quevedo, who was notary for the Council.[3] A royal *cedula* of October 12 definitively conferred the dignity upon Saavedra. The news came too late for him to include the honor on the title page of the first edition of *The Royal Politician*, but it appears in the Milan edition, dated 1642.

By the time the Diet adjourned in October, 1641, having accomplished little, Saavedra had already left. Since May he had been in Switzerland, having gone there at the request of the Parliament of Dôle to represent once again the interests of Franche-Comté in preserving a neutral position between France and the Empire. His experience was frustrating, as was almost every diplomatic effort that he made in the ensuing months, for the political tides of Europe had turned in favor of France.[4]

I   *In Support of the Spanish Cause*

Saavedra did not abandon his interest in the affairs of his beloved Franche-Comté even when, at the end of 1642 or beginning of 1643, he returned to Madrid. There he addressed a report, dated February 19, 1643, to Philip IV. In it he related the situation in the county of Burgundy.[5]

Scarcely had Saavedra arrived in Madrid when there occurred a momentous political event: Philip IV deposed his long-time favorite and prime minister, the Count-Duke of Olivares. The change did not seriously affect Saavedra at the time. He at last occupied his place on the Council of the Indies to which he had been named in

1635. In May he would be sixty years old, and he looked forward to
a few years of working at the seat of the monarchy which he had
represented abroad since he was a young man in his twenties.
Saavedra also continued his efforts in the propaganda war against
France. Sometime between January and March—that is, between
the fall of Olivares and the death of Louis XIII of France—he wrote
a tract entitled *Suspiros de Francia* (*Sighs of France*). It survives, in
a Spanish version, in a manuscript in the British Library. As in the
case of so much ephemeral literature of this period, we do not know
whether it was printed nor in what languages.[6]

Saavedra speaks with the voice of a personified France, who
prostrates herself at the feet of her monarch. "Do not be astonished
at my lugubrious garb," she tells him, "for, although your glorious
deeds crown my brow with laurel, the leaves are intertwined with
sorrowful twigs of cypress. Your victories have been written on the
pages of time not with ink but with the blood of my beloved sons.
The acclaims for your triumphs have been mingled with the lamen-
tation of parents for the death of their sons and the grief of brothers
for the demise of brothers" (p. 115).

As he had done in *Answer to the French Declaration* in 1635,
Saavedra pretended to express the point of view of a dissenting
Frenchman. The effort required of him was greater than eight years
before. By 1643 the French position was enormously strengthened,
and he was obliged to emphasize at what cost victory had been
bought, for he had to concede the victories. Knowing the author
and the circumstances, we detect the underlying pathos as Saavedra
stresses how much France needs the House of Austria as a buffer
against a Europe hostile to her.

But Saavedra's tract could not change the facts. The hostility of
Europe was effectively marshalled against Spain, and the course of
events was to make Saavedra's sojourn at court a short one. In the
late spring of 1643 news reached Madrid of the disastrous defeat of
Spanish arms near Rocroi, on the frontier between France and the
Spanish Netherlands. Spanish troops had laid siege to Rocroi, and
Louis de Bourbon, Duke of Enghien, later known as the Grand
Condé, came to the aid of the besieged town. On May 19, 1643, he
won a decisive victory over Spanish troops commanded by the
Count of Fontaine, a Lorrainer in the service of Spain. Of 26,000
Spanish soldiers, seven thousand lost their lives and many of the
survivors were badly wounded. It was a decisive victory in the long
struggle of France against Spain and the Empire for European
hegemony. Richelieu had died the year before, but his policies were
triumphant.

Spain must think of peace, and it was decided at Madrid to send a delegation to the congresses that were gathering in Westphalia. The Catholics were to meet in Münster, eighty miles northeast of Cologne; the Protestants in Osnabrück, another thirty miles northeast. Saavedra Fajardo, because of his years of experience in Italy and Germany, was a logical choice to be a Spanish representative, although he did not possess the titles of nobility later deemed necessary. The Council of State recommended him to Philip IV, who granted him plenipotentiary powers in a document dated July 11, 1643. Shortly afterward the sixty-year-old diplomat left Madrid bound for Münster. He traveled through France, for the plenipotentiary ministers to the Congress of Westphalia enjoyed special immunity. If he made any effort at official communication, the French were cool. When he passed through Paris, the queen mother and regent, Anne of Austria—the daughter of Philip III of Spain and mother of five-year-old Louis XIV—gave him only the time necessary to hear mass at the Carthusians, requiring him to depart from the city immediately afterward.[7]

In Brussels, in the Spanish Netherlands, Saavedra was obliged to make a long stay, for he fell seriously ill. His doctor was a Burgundian, Jean Jacques Chifflet (1588 - 1673), a native of Besançon in Franche-Comté and near Saavedra's age. He too had served in diplomatic missions, and Saavedra encouraged him in the writing of a book on which he was engaged, *Vindiciae Hispanicae* (*Spanish Claims*), which was published at Antwerp two years later, in 1645. During his convalescence Saavedra was in touch with men from the European "republic of letters" who were residing in Brussels or nearby at the time. Among them was the elderly and erudite Erycius Puteanus (Henri Dupuy in French, or van den Putte in Flemish; 1574 - 1646), the successor of the humanist Justus Lipsius in the chair of Latin language at the University of Louvain. In October, 1643, although he had not completely recovered, Saavedra continued his journey. At Cologne he met two colleagues who awaited him there, Antoine Brun, with whom he had served in the Diet at Regensburg, and Count Zapata. Traveling by land and by riverboat, they reached Münster on October 28, where the inhabitants received them with pomp and jubilation. Saavedra was beginning the most difficult and significant assignment of his diplomatic career.

An international congress for the establishment of "universal peace" had been repeatedly proposed for more than a decade. At last the ministers were assembling with the purpose of bringing to a close hostilities that had begun in 1618. But the representatives were slow in arriving at the two cities. Not until December, 1644, did the formal inauguration take place at Münster. Even so, the French ministers continued to delay, for that suited their purpose. In these circumstances, Saavedra Fajardo, still an active and temperamental man despite his recent illness, was impatient. One delegate wrote home about a love affair which he said occupied the Spanish abbé, but that story was likely malicious gossip. Saavedra found an outlet for his energies in propaganda. If he was to be frustrated in exercising the weapons of diplomacy against the cunning and evasive French, he could still carry on the struggle with the pen. To this period between October, 1643, and his departure for Madrid a little more than two years later, belong two of his last works, the dialogue *Locuras de Europa (The Folly of Europe)* and the monumental history *Corona gótica (Gothic Crown)*.

II *A Dialogue*

Although Saavedra was frustrated in initiating a diplomatic dialogue with the French, he did write a political and literary dialogue about them and the abominable events in Europe of which they, in his opinion, were the cause. The short work, *Folly of Europe*, is a conversation between Mercurio (the god Mercury) and Luciano, who is Lucian, the second-century Greek satirist who left us the classical models of the dialogue genre. Lucian had learned the form from Plato, so that the genre has its genesis in the very roots of Western literature.

The dialogue enjoyed in the sixteenth century a revival which persisted well into the seventeenth. The Dutch man of letters Desiderius Erasmus wrote what he called *formulae*, or model conversations, for students of Latin. In an age when the international language of Europe was Latin, schoolboys learned to speak the language as well as to read and write it; and Erasmus's model conversations were not unlike those that appear in foreign language texts today. However, they had a touch of his genius, and through a former colleague they came into the hands of a Basel printer who published them, to Erasmus's initial chagrin. The little book, *Familiarum Colloquiorum Formulae (Models of Familiar Conversations)* became a best seller, and Erasmus himself supervised later editions.

Erasmus also translated Lucian's Greek dialogues into Latin, and at the same time he expanded *Familiar Conversations* into the more elaborate book that we know today as the *Colloquies*.[8] The additions were addressed not so much to schoolboys as to young men. They retained the didactic purpose of teaching Latin, but they also instilled ideas, including anti-clerical ones. Their literary merit was such that they were attractive to adults as well as to youth, although the subjects, such as the series on love and marriage, were especially designed to appeal to young males. Saavedra, to be sure, affected disdain for Erasmus in *Republic of Letters*, comparing him to his disdavantage with scholastic theologians: "I saw Alexander of Hales and Duns Scotus making admirable trials of skill on the tightrope; but when Erasmus tried to imitate them . . . he fell flat on his face and set all the people gathered round to laughing."[9]

Other humanists followed Erasmus's example, although they tended to abandon the object of language learning in favor of disputation about ideas. The Spaniard Juan Luis Vives, professor at Louvain and Oxford, imitated in Latin the dialogues of his friend Erasmus. The brothers Juan and Alfonso de Valdés used the dialogue genre in Spanish for didactic purposes. Juan preserved a connection between the genre and language learning in *Diálogo de la lengua (Dialogue on Language)*, and his brother Alfonso used the dialogue to comment on current political events much as Saavedra was to do more than a century later. Alfonso's *Diálogo de Mercurio y Carón (Dialogue between Mercury and Charon)* relates events in the Franco-Spanish conflict of 1521 - 23, while the *Diálogo de las cosas ocurridas en Roma (Dialogue about Events in Rome)* deals with the sack of Rome in 1527 by the troops of Charles V, a circumstance viewed by Erasmists as divine punishment inflicted on the Church for its vice and wickedness. The summary of the dialogue, which the author placed at the beginning, reads as follows: "A young gentleman from the court of the Emperor, named Latancio, chances to meet in the square of Valladolid an archdeacon who has come from Rome in the uniform of a soldier. Going into the church of St. Francis, they speak about the events that occurred in Rome. In the first part, Latancio shows the archdeacon that the Emperor does not share in the blame for them, and in the second part he demonstrates that God permitted them to occur for the good of humanity."[10]

In the ensuing years, in all European countries, both in Latin and in the vernacular, the dialogue became a popular form of what was basically expository writing. Its growth corresponded to the development of the drama, which was also in dialogue form. In a time when new and radical ideas were being expounded, in an age when both civil and ecclesiastical authorities clapped men into jail for the expression of subversive ideas, the dialogue was an appropriate means of expression. As in the drama, the author disappeared behind his characters, who could indeed take different positions in the disputation. Furthermore, the dialogue had the additional advantage of presenting ideas in attractive garb; in the Spanish phrase, it could "deleitar enseñando," thus reaching a wider public. The ideas that Montaigne, for example, expounded in an essay for the select few could also be presented in a dialogue aimed at a wider audience. In fact, these dialogues can properly be thought of as belonging to an early branch of journalism, for, though issued irregularly, many of them came out as tracts or pamphlets rather than in full-length books. The dialogue had a notable vogue in France in the seventeenth century, and Saavedra probably chose this genre intentionally for the purpose of making political propaganda against France.[11]

Saavedra's dialogue begins with the meeting of Lucian and Mercury. "Where have you been, Mercury?" the Greek asks. "Your feet are wet, you are covered with dust, and your forehead is bathed in sweat. You're no credit to the gods. You gods are not supposed to suffer pain and anguish."[12] We imagine the winged messenger panting and wiping his brow as he replies: "The world is in such a state that it makes even us gods sweat." Lucian tells him he has no one to blame but himself if he left the tranquility of the heavens to go down to earth at a time when its inhabitants "hate life and are bent on separating their bodies from their souls." Mercury confesses that curiosity took him to earth. He had to see for himself whether the folly of men was as great as he had been told by Justice, Truth, Faith, and Modesty, who had come to dwell in heaven because they could not bear to live on earth.

Thus the stage is set for a far-ranging commentary on the ills of Europe. Mercury has seen events that are hard to believe. "I have viewed some things with anguish because of the sufferings of the people; other things have provoked me to laughter because of the ignorance of those who govern them" (p. 1198). Having toured all of Europe, the god remained suspended in the air above to take it all in. "Everywhere I saw blood-drenched War." And now hiding behind the character Mercury, Saavedra begins the attack on France: "I saw some nations doing battle with others because of the whim and for the benefit of one nation alone, which continually fans the flames of war."

Mercury then expounds what will be the thesis of the whole dialogue. Europe is mad not to recognize that its felicity lies in defense of the just positions of the House of Austria, and the continent is foolish not to see that support of France has brought on ruin.

I wondered at Europe's folly [Mercury says] in abandoning the blessings of peace, the sweet pleasures of the homeland, and the undisturbed possession of one's own property, in order to embark on the conquest of other places. How silly it is for men to capture other towns when there are not enough people to fill their own. They destroy and burn the very lands, towns, and cities that they want to acquire. They risk their lives and property in order that this or that crown may secure another span of land. Their soldiers assault a town where they will neither dwell nor even rest for a day after it is taken, because the ambition of their princes dazzles them with thoughts of glory and honor, for which shining but insubstantial coin they boldly sell themselves to the Grim Reaper (p. 1199).

From this point on, with Lucian drawing him out, Mercury gets down to the details of Europe's ills. He has a poor opinion of Münster and Osnabrück as sites for the peace conferences. Situated in the midst of the conflict itself, they serve as a base from which the delegates can embroil themselves in the dissension. "Peace is on the lips of the ministers, but war lies in their hearts and bursts from their pens" (p. 1200). Indeed, in the course of the dialogue, Mercury and Lucian talk about half a dozen pamphlets that the French have circulated to further their political aims.

As Mercury surveyed the countries of Europe, he was puzzled at the indifference of Poland to the dangers that threatened her frontiers. Sweden, triumphant during its incursions into the German states, has blindly allied herself with France and appears ignorant of the true designs of that perfidious nation. Holland has helped Sweden in her attack on Denmark, not recognizing that if Sweden dominates Denmark, she will be in a position to close the Baltic to Dutch commerce. France, too, is deceiving the Dutch by persuading them to help her conquer Dunkirk; and the treacherous French try to convince the Dutch that once France possesses Flanders and borders on the Low Countries, the latter will flourish because of their proximity to France.

In this vein the two interlocutors range across the whole spectrum of European politics. Although England figured little in European affairs during these years—the 1640's were a period of internal strife as Cromwell and Parliament challenged royal power—Mercury and Lucian touch upon events there, the conflicts with the Scots and the Irish, and the tactics of the recently deceased Richelieu in fomenting discord between English and Scots. The two also blame Richelieu for encouraging that disaffection among Catalans and Portuguese that led to the separatist movements of those years. Lucian states succinctly the Castilian attitude toward the Portuguese problem:

The Portuguese ought not to object to the union of their crown with that of Castile. Portugal left Spain as a county and she has returned as a kingdom, not to be incorporated or absorbed into Spain again but rather to flourish side by side with it. Nor can the Portuguese say that they have a foreign king. He is their own, for he came into possession of the kingdom not by conquest but by the legitimate succession of fathers and sons; and he has been governing Portugal under its own laws, customs, and language, not as if the people were Castilians . . . (p. 1211).

The discussion on Catalonia is extensive. The two speakers take turns refuting statements in a book by an anonymous Frenchman entitled *Catalonia Is French*. Like Besian Arroy, the author established French claims to Catalonia beginning with Charlemagne and carried them to the present day. He also demonstrated that Catalans would be better off under France than under Spain.

Finally, Mercury and Lucian return to the direct assault on France. Mercury believes he saw many signs of weakness in that country: the minority of the king, government by a woman (the queen mother), the prime ministership invested in a foreigner (Mazarin, Richelieu's successor), the conflicts between Council and Parliament, discontent and distrust of the government among the people, the diversity of religion, lack of men and money, and oppressive taxation. "How then," Lucian asks, "do you explain that France can field so many armies and sustain so many wars?" Mercury's answer suggests one of the great miscalculations of history: "These are France's dying efforts, similar to the light of a candle, which flares up when its substance is exhausted and the flame is about to go out" (p. 1216).

Did Saavedra believe his own propaganda? Probably not. But he wanted to sow seeds of doubt in the minds of those like Duke Maximilian of Bavaria, who were wavering between support of Spain, or simple neutrality, and alliance with the French. And he could hope against hope. The signs of weakness in France were there. Yet such was the vigor of the country that it surmounted the ineptness of its government to enter boldly into its "Grand Siècle." Saavedra, like many a political commentator before and after him, may have erred because he saw what he wanted to see. *Folly of Europe* is not clairvoyant; it is propaganda; it is a political tract.

Did Saavedra print *Folly of Europe?* Did he circulate it in some manner so that it served its purpose as propaganda? If so, in what language? We do not know the answers to these questions. We can only conjecture that he intended for it to circulate, and that it would have been more effective in a language other than Spanish. Perhaps a scholar studying the history of the Thirty Years' War will some day discover a version of it in Latin, or French, or Dutch, or German.

The known facts of its publication are these. The Spanish text that we possess appeared in print in 1748, exactly one hundred years after the conclusion of the Peace of Westphalia and on the centennial of Saavedra's death. The title page gives the date, but it does not give either the printer or the place of publication. Vicente Salvá believed that it was printed in Germany.[13] The title page calls it a posthumous work of Saavedra, gives his titles including that of plenipotentiary to the Congress of Münster, and states that it was printed from a "manuscript copy."

A few years later Antonio Valladares de Sotomayor published it in his magazine *Semanario Erudito (Scholarly Weekly;* VI, 1 - 44), in a number which appeared in 1787. He took it from a manuscript that belonged to the Duke of Híjar. From the magazine, the text entered the Madrid, 1819, edition of Saavedra's works and the volume of his works in the Biblioteca de Autores Españoles. Reprints have been based on one of these sources. No critical edition has been made.

III   *The Gothic Kings of Spain*

The enforced leisure that Saavedra enjoyed in Münster resulted in another book, *Corona gótica (Gothic Crown)*, an historical work of major proportions compared with *Folly of Europe.* He says in the preface, with some exaggeration, "as the days and months and years passed without my being able to advance our negotiations—for reasons known to all—I felt obliged to work at something that would advance the cause of our king. . . ."[14] The project was three times vaster than Saavedra was able to realize, for the title page of the first edition, which is dated Münster, 1646, reads: *Corona gótica, castellana y austriaca (Gothic, Castilian, and Austrian Crown).* It was Saavedra's intention, therefore, to write a history of the Castilian and Austrian kings of Spain as well as of the Gothic kings.

Gothic Crown has thirty chapters, each devoted, in chronological order, to one, two, or three Gothic kings—thirty-six in all. Saavedra begins with Alaric I (370? - 410), who plundered the Rome of the

Emperor Honorius but never got to Spain; and Ataulphus (d. 415), who married Honorius's half sister Galla Placidia, led an army into Spain, and was assassinated in Barcelona; and so on through all those Gothic kings with the barbaric names—Walia, Eurico, Atanagildo, Hermenegildo, Recaredo, Sisebuto, Wamba—that have been the bane of generations of Spanish school children. He concludes with the chapter on Roderick, the last Gothic king, whose concupiscence, according to legend, brought on the Moorish invasion from Africa. (He seduced Florinda, daughter of Count Julián; in revenge the count, whose lands were located along the Strait of Gibraltar, invited the Moors to invade Spain through his territory.)

Writing at Münster at a time when Spain was the victim of vicious propaganda and when he himself engaged his pen in counterattacks, Saavedra could not help but place history at the service of his country. The French said that he wrote *Gothic Crown* to attract the Swedes to the side of the House of Austria by showing the common origin of the two crowns. This was quite possibly true, for Saavedra was friendly with Rosenham, the Swedish ambassador; and diplomatic gossip said that he had proposed an alliance with the Protestant Swedes based on the marriage of Philip IV and Queen Christina of Sweden, whose Roman Catholic sympathies were suspected although she had not yet embraced that faith.[15] Even from the point of view of propaganda, however, Saavedra's purpose is broader. He says in his preface to the reader that there was scarcely a part of the Spanish monarchy to which other nations did not lay claim. This fact was hindering the conclusion of peace and even making it impossible. He aimed, therefore, in this historical work, to show the legitimate rights which the Spanish crown had to hold its territories (p. 709).

Saavedra's concept is, however, more comprehensive. When he wrote *Introduction to Political Science*, which is abstract, he followed it with *Statecraft of King Ferdinand the Catholic*, which is concrete. The second part served to illustrate the first. *Gothic Crown* bears a similar relationship to *The Royal Politician*. In the dedication to Prince Baltasar Carlos (whose death came just thirteen months after Saavedra wrote it), the author said: "In *The Royal Politician* I demonstrated the theory of statecraft for Your Highness, and now I offer its practice as revealed in the lives of the Gothic kings of Spain . . . " (p. 705). Saavedra openly declared his didactic intent to the young prince: "I beg Your Highness to observe those things which made some of these kings glorious and beloved, and, on the contrary, those other things which took from them their good fame, their scepters, and their lives . . ." (p. 705).

In effect, Saavedra sought in the life of each king a moral lesson. Each chapter begins with a reflection.[16] The reign of Teodorico II (454 - 467) shows the origins of tyranny (Chap. VII). The life of Agila (reigned 549 - 553) demonstrates the dangers of ambition (Chap. XIII). It begins:

Human ambition is unable to judge properly the positions to which it can rightly aspire. Blinded by glittering honors, a man hungers for the highest post and fails to assess the danger he incurs when, for lack of courage and prudence, he cannot meet its demands. For this reason many people are failures in public positions although they were successful in private life. That is what happened to Agila when he was elected king of the Goths. He turned out to be inept at government, and the crown soon fell from his head. He expected to find happiness in the possession of it; but he met his death (p. 846).

However, Saavedra's concept of history is not entirely distorted by his moral preoccupations. He himself wrote that the first purpose of history is to tell and secondarily to teach.[17] But the tale has meaning. History is to a nation what memory is to a person. Thus it has a practical as well as a moral value. It serves a pragmatic and exemplary purpose by supplying material on which human understanding and prudence may work. "Posterity is governed by the examples of history which it should either imitate or avoid; from history a government derives facts and principles for the rule of its kingdom . . ." (p. 800). An historical theorist, Luis Cabrera de Córdoba, who considered history the collective memory of man's experience on this earth, said of it: "History does not mean writing things down so that they are not forgotten . . . but so that they may teach us to use experience; it is a silent teacher which individuals use to perfect their prudence."[18]

In the development of Spanish historiography, Saavedra Fajardo's *Gothic Crown* represents a transition. His writing is colored by that desire felt so strongly by the writer of emblems to dress up morality so that it will be as attractive as vice. Thus Saavedra's history is dramatic and novelesque. He brings in Spain's rich legendary material, such as the picturesque elements of the story of Roderick, the last Gothic king, and adds elements of his own invention. He composes a letter that the violated Florinda supposedly wrote. Roderick and Tarif deliver harangues before battle. Because of such recourses as these Saavedra belongs to the rhetorical school of the past. However, he also anticipates, through his use of a great variety of sources, the erudite school which some thirty years later was to flower in the works of the Marquis of Mondéjar, Nicolás Antonio, and Father José de Moret.[19]

The sources for *Gothic Crown* are many. Saavedra cites more than four hundred authors, Spanish and foreign, ancient and modern. Marginal notes abound and are often long.[20] With Baroque metaphors he defends his use of them: "Since the accounts of those centuries are obscure and confused, it has been appropriate in this history to open windows along the margins in order to let the light come in. There I have shown the elements I have used in writing it, which are not unlike the varicolored stones or the feathers of different birds from which an image is composed . . ." (p. 708). Saavedra considered his work was well along toward completion when he mentioned it by its full title in a letter to Philip IV in May, 1644 (*Epistolario,* p. 1380). However, he wrote the dedication more than a year later, and *Gothic Crown,* the first part, issued from the press of "Juan Jansonio"—the printer's name is Hispanicized on the title page—at Münster early in 1646.

The first part contained only the Gothic kings and ended with the year 714. In the prologue Saavedra says that the second part is "very far along" (p. 708). However, he never published it. By May of 1646 he had returned to Madrid, and he never got back to his history. A second part did appear, however, in 1671, twenty-three years after Saavedra's death. It was "composed of some originals left by Don Diego Saavedra Fajardo," as the title page says, and was "continued by Don Alonso Núñez de Castro." The historical period covered was 714 to 1216.

Núñez de Castro was the son of a physician who served Philip IV. The year Saavedra died, 1648, he published a book with an unwieldy title that nevertheless reveals interests similar to Saavedra's: *Espejo cristalino de armas para generales valerosos, de desengaños para cristianos príncipes . . . (The Glass Mirror: Weapons for Valiant Generals and Sad Lessons of Experience for Christian Princes . . .).* Ten years later, in 1658, he published another book with a title that was proverbial in Spain and its empire: *Solo Madrid es Corte (Madrid Is the Only Court).* The bibliographer Nicolás Antonio lists other works by Núñez, who became a royal chronicler.[21]

In the prologue to the reader Núñez explains that he acquired some of Saavedra's originals from a friend, the Jesuit Father Juan Antonio Velázquez. He does not say how Velázquez happened to have them. He attempted to locate other "notebooks" that he knew were missing, but he could not find them. Núñez's second part covers the period from 714 to 1216, that is, from the reign of Pelayo up to that of Fernando III the Saint, a total of thirty-three kings. Thirteen chapters, covering nineteen kings, are by Saavedra Fajardo. In marginal notes Núñez indicates the sections that are Saavedra's and those that are his own. In the *Complete Works* (1946) González Palencia has published only those chapters that are from Saavedra's pen.

In all, Núñez published four parts: the first entirely by Saavedra, the second in which he collaborated posthumously with Saavedra, and the third and fourth, which are wholly his own with no material by Saavedra. The biographies became more detailed as he approached what would have then seemed more recent times. The third part (1677) covered the reigns of but four kings who ruled from 1217 to 1312: Fernando III the Saint, Alfonso X the Wise, Sancho the Brave, and Fernando IV. The fourth part (licensed 1683) deals with three kings—Alfonso XI, Pedro the Cruel, and Enrique II—who reigned from 1312 to 1379. Thus Núñez did not reach the period of the Austrian crown, and Saavedra's grandiose project remained incomplete.

In the same letter in which Saavedra wrote that the *Gothic, Castilian, and Austrian Crown* was near completion—he may have meant only the first part, to be sure—he gave the title of another book "which I have completed and ready for the press" (*Epistolario*, p. 1380). Its title was *Guerras y movimientos de Italia, de cuarenta años a esta parte (Wars and Uprisings in Italy in the Last Forty Years)*. It must be listed among his lost works.

IV *The Correspondence (Epistolario)*

No scholar has made a concerted effort to collect the correspondence of Saavedra Fajardo. Over the years, however, a number of his letters have been published. In 1853 the Biblioteca de Autores Españoles (Vol. 25) printed five. The year 1884, the tercentenary of his birth, marked a renewal of Saavedra studies. The Count of Roche and José Pío Tejera printed twelve letters in their book *Saavedra Fajardo: sus pensamientos, sus poesías, sus opúsculos*, which was the point of departure for modern studies. Five of them were the same ones that had appeared in the B. A. E., but six came from the General Archive at Simancas and one from the files of the city government of Murcia. That same year the Colección de Documentos Inéditos para la Historia de España

(Collection of Unpublished Documents for the History of Spain), which had included one letter in Vol. 47, printed a large number in Vol. 82.[22] They pertain to the years 1643 - 48 and especially to the Peace Congress in Westphalia. In 1891 the Duchess of Berwick and Alba published a single letter.[23]

González Palencia in the *Complete Works* (1946) includes all these among the 119 items that he calls Saavedra's *Epistolario* (*Collected Letters*), and he adds others. However, among the items he printed are extracts of Saavedra's correspondence made for the Council of State rather than the letters themselves, the texts of two treaty agreements with the Princess of Mantua, his last will and testament, and discourses, so that the number of letters is really but 104. A single extract referring to the months of October and November, 1633, refers to twenty-four letters sent to the Count-Duke of Olivares and to Philip IV, as well as copies of others directed to the Cardinal-Infante Don Fernando, the Count of Oñate, and the Duke of Feria. This suggests that the number of letters that are lost, undiscovered, or unpublished must be very great indeed. González Palencia mentions that the historian Antonio Ballesteros had seen original letters of Saavedra Fajardo in the Vienna archives, but in the period before 1946 when Palencia was preparing the *Complete Works* he could not have access to them (pp. 1283 - 84).

In an outstanding study of Saavedra the diplomat, Fraga Iribarne published a list of references to him in the archives of the Spanish Embassy at the Vatican; the list includes letters.[24] Fraga also worked in the Archives at Munich, which contain many letters. He used this correspondence in writing his book, and he published some of the letters or selected passages from them in the footnotes or in the text. Those letters that were written in Italian he translated into Spanish. In the Archives du Doubs (Franche-Comté) there are also letters by Saavedra that Fraga prints in part in his text and notes. In the area of Saavedra's correspondence much still remains to be done, for like other outstanding figures of Spanish history and literature, scholarship has not served Saavedra well.

Clearly most of Saavedra's correspondence belongs to diplomatic history, and its value lies in the documentary evidence that it provides. However, much of it possesses a texture that marks it as the work of a literary man. One of the earliest letters is written from Rome to the Canon Don Fernando Camaño in Santiago de Compostela. Saavedra had worked hard to secure from the Congregation of Rites the privilege of weekly prayers to St. James in the

Cathedral at Santiago. He himself had been appointed canon there, and he wanted to collect the money from his benefice without living in Santiago. He had, he felt, worked in Rome on behalf of the Cathedral, and he wanted some recompense from the Galicians, who had a reputation for being tight-fisted: "Your agent will inform you," he wrote Camaño, "how hard I have toiled and the money and effort I have put into this job. So don't you people act like Galicians with me. Send me the income from my benefice" (*Epistolario*, p. 1286).

When the Marchioness of Carpio wrote Cardinal Borja soliciting the vacant deanship of the Cathedral at Seville for her candidate, the negotiations were committed to Saavedra's care. He wrote the marchioness describing his success: "I threw myself at the feet of His Holiness, and I did not get up until he granted me the decree . . ." (p. 1286).

In 1631 Saavedra wrote to a representative of the city government at Murcia describing in vivid language the Lombardy canal, which made use of locks to lift boats from one level to another. His enthusiasm led him to imagine that a canal might be constructed from Murcia to Orihuela and thence to Guardamar and the sea (pp. 1287 - 88). The letter is a curious antecedent of that enlightened eighteenth-century interest in canal building which invaded Spain from other European countries.

Some of the phrases that were picked up in the extracts of Saavedra's correspondence make us hope that the originals will be discovered. Shortly after arriving at the court of Bavaria he sent Olivares a letter dated October 6, 1633, which, according to the extract "reports the gifts of amber, lengths of cloth, and other presents for madame [the duchess] and her ladies, and how well received were these gifts because of the avaricious nature of the Germans, which lets them be easily won over by these means" (*Epistolario*, pp. 1303 - 4). In a November letter, according to the extract, "Don Diego says that the astrologers have foretold a very bloody victory for [the Duke of Mecklenburg] in December, and that an old man of the city of Deggendorf predicted that the King of Sweden, seeing the city in turmoil, would not occupy it; but that another enemy would come and take it, and, then entering into the Passau area, would be defeated" (p. 1305). The Council of State dryly commented: "Acknowledge receipt of his letter and tell him not to believe in astrologers henceforth" (p. 1307).

The letters from Bavaria reflect the vigor with which Saavedra approached those years of diplomatic combat. In contrast, the cor-

respondence from Münster reveals the defeatism that was invading
the Spanish monarchy. There is poignancy in Saavedra's expression
of Spanish impotence to stop the French advance on every front.
The French had won on the battlefield at Rocroi. They are also win-
ning the war of propaganda, and no small part of their effectiveness
lay in the ostentatious display of wealth that they staged for the
benefit of the Germans. Anne of Austria, the queen of France—that
erstwhile Spanish princess—insisted that the delegates to the
Westphalia congress should be called ministers plenipotentiary.
Saavedra wrote plaintively to Don Jerónimo Villanueva in Madrid:

. . . it would have been preferable for us [not to be called plenipoten-
tiaries], because we would be less obliged to put on a show of wealth. I have
been forced to go into debt several thousand ducats, and I don't know what
to expect in the future, because I see no way to keep up with my expenses. I
can't even spend a *real* to pay for information or to push ahead with our
business. The negotiations here are viewed as of the utmost importance by
everyone, so that I don't understand how His Majesty can let matters stand
as they are. The French do not stint themselves. Even before they arrived
they had distributed various sums of money to win over the officials of the
city. So that you will understand how we live here and what will be
necessary to keep us going in the most expensive city in Germany, I am
obliged to tell you that I keep two coaches with red velvet upholstery and
with two teams of six horses each, six saddle horses, a litter with mules, six
pages, four lackeys, and eight chamberlains. Everything else is on that
scale; for example, my house is well furnished with tapestries. Count
Zapata's expenses are of the same magnitude. Even so, we cannot compete
with the French, who, as everyone remarks, live amidst great pomp. For
many months now they have had thirty horses and many servants . . . (p.
1363).

Thus in March, 1644, Saavedra enjoyed parity with the French as
far as horses were concerned: he had thirty horses and so did they.
Less than a month later Count Zapata was dead, and Saavedra
wrote to King Philip himself:

We don't know the cause of his illness, but it is attributed to overwhelming
feelings of sadness and melancholy. He was burdened with many expenses
and had not the means to pay for them. We are under constant threat of an
incident, because a large number of French, Portuguese, and Catalans have
entered the city, and we Spaniards are relatively few and our lodgings are
separated. Sir, I cannot insist too much that it is not in your best interests to
send to this Congress, exposed to the eyes of the world, ministers who are to
make a peace treaty but who do not have a *real* with which to support
themselves. We haven't the money to dispatch a messenger or pay for any

other service on behalf of Your Majesty. The King of France has sent plenipotentiaries each and every one of whom have perquisites, expense accounts, and twenty thousand ducats in salary a year. Today M. Avaux told me he had sixty horses here. I should tell you that the plenipotentiaries who represent princes are treated here like ambassadors with no difference at all. M. Avaux and M. Servien, although they are private ministers accountable to Longueville, who is the principal envoy, even have canopies in their houses and they put up seats of honor in the churches. We follow a modest course although in our public appearances we try to maintain a gravity worthy of servants of Your Majesty by ceding nothing to the other ministers. But it will be impossible to sustain appearances and expenses any longer in the most expensive city in Germany. When the French arrived, prices doubled. I am in debt more than five thousand ducats, and I should like to have a greater fortune in order to use it for the benefit of Your Majesty . . . (p. 1369).

Obviously, the correspondence of Saavedra belongs principally to the fields of history and biography. Yet his ardent nature and his commitment to the particular task at hand impart to his letters a character that entitles some of them to a niche in literature.

V   *Conclusion*

We may see the ministers plenipotentiary of whom Saavedra wrote in the canvas by Gerard Terborch (1617 - 1681) that hangs in the museum at Münster.[25] The painter went as a young man of twenty-nine from Amsterdam to the city in Westphalia, drawn there with the hope of profiting from the peace conference. In the foreground his picture shows a dozen figures at full-length or almost so, while we see the heads of more than thirty others ranged behind them. Most of the plenipotentiaries have their hair parted in the middle and falling to shoulder length. Many are mustachioed and wear slight Vandyke beards. The recumbent effigy on a tomb seen in the middle ground enhances the tone of gravity and dignity, as does a crucifix dimly visible high in the background. Most of the men in the foreground wear clerical cassocks with falling band collars or reduced ruff. Prominently in the left foreground, however, stands a fashionable figure in doublet, jerkin, and breeches, a spotted dog at his heels. In one gloved hand he holds a dashing, plumed hat; in the other a walking stick. On his feet he wears boots with extremely wide tops folded down and then up again. Seen in profile facing the other figures, he seems to represent the new secular Europe that confronts the clerical world from which most of the others come. Our eyes are drawn to him again and

again. He is the new man in the Europe of Louis XIV, of an independent Netherlands, of the Restoration that was to be in
England.

Spain could count few friends among those portrayed, clerical or
lay. Terborch's painting is a picture of Europe—Catholic Europe
for the most part, because the Protestants were at Osnabrück—
ranged against Counter-Reformation Spain. What Protestant
England had begun in 1588, the year of the defeat of the Spanish
Armada, Protestant and Catholic Europe, in alliance, were pressing
to an end in 1648. The aim was to crush Spanish hegemony in
Europe, pushing Spanish power back to the Peninsula where the
Catalans and Portuguese also sought to reduce it in their areas. The
object was nearly achieved in 1648; it became definitive with the
Peace of the Pyrenees in 1659. The next year Velázquez accompanied the Infanta María Teresa to the Isle of Pheasants in the
Bidasoa River, where she married the young Sun King. A Spanish
princess again shared the French throne, but the rest of that century
and the next belonged to a secular France, a prosperous, commercial Netherlands, and to an imperial England that emerged from
the Puritan Revolution.

Saavedra did not stay for the final signing of the peace treaties.
He left Münster in 1646, when he was succeeded by Don Gaspar de
Bracamonte y Guzmán, Count of Peñaranda. By May of that year
he was back in Madrid where he took up again his work in the
Council of the Indies. It was appropriate, too, that a man who had
spent so many years abroad should be appointed to introduce ambassadors. It was also fitting tht the author of *Republic of Letters*
should be called upon to serve as a censor. On September 4, 1647,
the man who had planned to write *Gothic, Castilian, and Austrian
Crown* signed the approval for printing a biography of Pedro the
Cruel, *El Rey D. Pedro defendido (King Don Pedro Defended)* by
Juan Antonio de Vera y Figueroa.[26] Although Saavedra owned a
house in the Calle del Pez (Fish Street), he preferred to reside nearby at St. Anthony's Hospital, which Philip III had founded as a
residence for Portuguese who lived at court. For his old age
Saavedra remodeled an apartment in the Convent of Augustinian
Recollects, then on the outskirts of Madrid where the National
Library now stands on Recoletos Boulevard. He did not live to occupy those quarters. He fell ill in August, 1648. He made his will on
the 13th, and on the 24th he died. He was buried in the convent.

Saavedra Fajardo enjoyed a modest but worthy posthumous fame
in the world of European letters. Throughout the rest of the

seventeenth century and the whole of the eighteenth *The Royal Politician* and *Republic of Letters* were reprinted and translated. The Verdussen firm in Antwerp kept Saavedra's works in print in Spanish in handsome quarto volumes for three quarters of a century. The Royal Spanish Academy named him an authority on the use of the Spanish language in its six-volume dictionary of 1726 - 39 and quoted extensively from his principal works. The last important edition of this long period came in 1819 with the four-volume set done by the García press in Madrid. In the Romantic age his fame suffered a brief eclipse, but the B. A. E. volume of 1853 made his collected works again readily available. Then two young Murcians, the Count of Roche and José Pío Tejera, began his modern rehabilitation in 1884, the tercentenary of his birth. His position in Spanish letters was definitively reestablished by the essays of Azorín.

During the tumult of the early years of the nineteenth century, the French invaders sacked the Augustinian convent on Recoletos Boulevard, and the plaque on Saavedra's tomb disappeared. The Augustinians opened the crypt on their return, and the bones of the great thinker were put in a box and kept among the convent's relics. The Marquis of Molíns tells the story of an English tourist who visited the convent with his son. Taking Saavedra's skull, he placed it in his son's hands. "Hold this, my boy," he said, "so that when you return home you may say that you have touched with your own hands the cranium of the first statesman of this nation and one of the greatest minds of his century."[27]

The subsequent fate of Saavedra's bones brings to mind once again the engraving that illustrates the closing poem, "Ludibria Mortis," in *The Royal Politician*. In the graphic we see, amidst fallen, shattered columns, a cobwebbed skull resting on a crumbling foundation of bricks and stone. The nineteenth-century prior of the Augustinian convent, realizing that the bones of a former diplomat did not properly belong among the convent's relics of saints, ordered them to be kept in his own cell. However, the sexton much admired the handsome skull, and he got permission to use it and the two shinbones to decorate the catafalques at funeral services in the convent.

In 1835 the Mendizábal government decreed the confiscation of church property, confirming actions that had already been going on, for in 1834 Mendizábal himself had come into possession of the choice location of the Augustinians on Recoletos Boulevard. The buildings were converted to use as a garage for the repair of

carriages and a wax museum, the Galería Topográfica y Pin-
toresca.[28] The former sexton of the convent lent or sold Saavedra's
skull to the owner of the museum. The latter placed it in the hands
of a penitent Mary Magdalene who stood between the effigies of
the bull-fighter Francisco Montes and the goddess Venus.
Academicians of the Academy of History, alarmed at this disposition of Saavedra's cranium, took legal steps and came into possession of the skull and shinbones and also learned that the rest of his
remains were lost beyond recovery. For a time the surviving bones
were kept on a shelf at the Academy's building in León Street, and
then they were moved to the royal church of San Isidro. There, in
1883, the Murcian Don Javier Fuentes y Ponte, found them,
covered with dust and spider webs, lying on a chair in a closet in the
old sacristy.[29] The skull had the name "Sabedra" written on it. At
Fuente's urging, the diocese and the municipal council of Murcia
petitioned the Academy of History for the return of Saavedra's
bones to his native province. The request was granted, and the next
year, 1884, on the tercentenary of his birth, Saavedra's surviving
bones were moved to Murcia and deposited in the cathedral.

Today, in the nearby village of Algezares, where he was born, a
bust of Saavedra stands in a small park at a fork in the road. Behind
him rise the jagged scorched ridges of the sawtooth range that cuts
the Iberian blue sky: the Cresta del Gallo, the Cock's Comb. High
on a mountain above is the Sanctuary of Our Lady of Fuensanta,
which was founded in 1610—about the time Saavedra first went to
Rome—by the repentant actors María de Gracia and Juan Bautista
Gómez. Nearby is the monastery of Our Lady of Light, into which
Cardinal Belluga, at the beginning of the eighteenth century,
gathered the many hermits who lived in caves and huts on the
mountainside. Saavedra's bust looks out over the Murcian plain
where green truck gardens contrast with the austere background. In
the fertile irrigated bottomland of the Segura River, orange and
lemon groves and market gardens flourish as do poultry and pig
farms. Beyond this prosperous agricultural scene, on the opposite
bank of the river, rises the city of Murcia, dominated by the
Cathedral of Santa María where Saavedra's skull and shinbones at
last came to rest.

In the spirit of the man whose life and works were devoted to the
conservation of Christian government in a secular world, I close using the words with which he ended the last prose essay that preceded the final poem of *The Royal Politician*,

LAUS DEO.

Notes and References

The following abbreviations are used in the notes and in the bibliography:

B. A. E.   Biblioteca de Autores Españoles
B. N. M.   Biblioteca Nacional, Madrid
CODOIN Colección de Documentos Inéditos para la Historia de España
C. S. I. C. Consejo Superior de Investigaciones Científicas
R   Rare Book Collection, B. N. M.

Preface

1. Miguel de Cervantes Saavedra, *The Ingenious Gentleman Don Quixote de la Mancha*, trans., Samuel Putnam (New York: The Viking Press, 1949), II, 505 (Prologue to Part II). Subsequent references in the text are to Parts I or II and to chapter (applicable to any edition), while page numbers refer to this edition. I have sometimes preferred my own versions, but I have taken into account the Putnam translation, which I cite with permission of The Viking Press.

2. John Dowling, "Saavedra Fajardo's *República literaria:* The Bibliographical History of Little Masterpiece (Part III)," *Hispanófila* 23, No. 69 (1980).

3. William H. Roberts, "Juan Guerrero Ruiz (1893 - 1955)," *Revista Hispánica Moderna* 22 (1956), 1 - 4.

Chapter One

1. Diego de Saavedra Fajardo, *Sus pensamientos, sus poesías, sus opúsculos*, ed. Conde de Roche and José Pío Tejera (Madrid, 1884), p. xxviii.

2. Justo García Soriano, "Introducción" to Francisco Cascales, *Cartas filológicas* (Madrid, 1930), I, 18.

3. Justo García Soriano, *El humanista Francisco Cascales* (Madrid, 1924), p. 242.

4. Ibid., pp. 44 - 45.

5. Quoted by Francisco de Bizagorena [Francisco Tamames], *Salamanca: su historia, su arte, su cultura* (Madrid, 1964), p. 71.

6. José Camón Aznar, *Salamanca (guía artística)* (Salamanca, 1953), p. 82.

7. Local tradition to this day rejects scholarship. M. Herrero García, "Notas sobre *La Celestina*," *Revista de Filología Española* 11 (1924): 402 - 12, supports the claims of Toledo over those of Salamanca.

8. My references are to the translation by Samuel Putnam, *The Ingenious Gentleman Don Quixote de la Mancha* (New York: The Viking Press, 1949), 2 vols. In order that other editions may be used, the numbers in parentheses are to Parts I or II, to chapter, and then to page.

9. Cited by Henry Kamen, *The Spanish Inquisition* (New York, 1969), p. 94.

10. Walter Poesse, *Juan Ruiz de Alarcón* (New York, 1972), pp. 13 - 14.

11. Quoted by Angel Valbuena Prat, *La vida española en la edad de oro* (Barcelona, 1943), p. 49.

12. José Martínez Ruiz, "Saavedra Fajardo," in *De Granada a Castelar* (Madrid, 1922), pp. 121 - 22.

13. My translations follow an eighteenth-century English text but I have modified them as I have thought necessary: *Respublica Literaria, or The Republick of Letters, Being a Vision*. Wrote in Spanish by Don Diego de Saavedra, Knight of the Order of St. James. Translated from the Original by J. E., A. B. (London, 1727), p. 2. Subsequent page references are given in the text.

14. Diego de Saavedra Fajardo, *República literaria*, ed. José de Salinas; prologue, Francisco Ignacio de Porres (Alcalá de Henares, 1670), [60] + 159 pp.

15. Vicente García de Diego, "Prólogo" to Diego de Saavedra Fajardo, *República literaria* (Madrid, 1956), p. xlix. Hansgerd Schulte studies *desengaño* chiefly in prose works in *El desengaño: Wort und Thema in der spanischen Literatur des Goldenen Zeitalters* (München, 1969); while Margaret Van Antwerp Norris deals with the counter theme, especially in poetry, in "The Rejection of *Desengaño*: A Counter Tradition in Golden Age Poetry," *Revista Hispánica Moderna* 36 (1970 - 71): 9 - 20.

16. Ruth Lundelius, "Skepticism in Saavedra Fajardo's *República literaria*," a paper read at the convention of the South Atlantic Modern Language Association, Nov. 7, 1975; abstract in *South Atlantic Bulletin* 41, No.1 (1975): 87.

17. Final paragraph of the prologue (page not numbered).

18. García de Diego, "Prólogo," p. lii.

19. Claudio Antonio de Cabrera, pseud. for Diego de Saavedra Fajardo, *Juicio de artes y ciencias* (Madrid, 1655), unnumbered preliminary pages.

20. John Milton, *Areopagitica and Of Education*, ed. George H. Sabine (New York, 1951), p. 50.

21. García de Diego, "Prólogo," pp. liii - liv. A Spanish version may be found in Juan Luis Vives, *Obras completas*, trans. Lorenzo Ribera (Madrid, 1947), I, 277 - 83.

22. Marguerite Ruth Lundelius, "A Comparative Study of the *Vanity of the Arts and Sciences* by Henry Cornelius Agrippa and the *República literaria* by Diego de Saavedra Fajardo," unpublished M. A. thesis, The University of Texas, 1954, 70 pp.

23. Lundelius, pp. 28 - 29.

24. Lundelius, pp. 51 - 64.

25. John Dowling, "Saavedra Fajardo's *República literaria:* The Bibliographical History of a Little Masterpiece," Parts I, II, and III, *Hispanófila* 23, Nos. 67, 68, and 69 (1979 - 80).

26. Jonathan Swift, *Gulliver's Travels,* introduction by Jacques Barzun (New York: Crown Publishers, 1947), pp. 222 and 224.

27. Annie Barnes, *Jean Le Clerc (1657 - 1736) et la République des Lettres* (Paris, 1938), pp. 13, 16, 17 et passim.

28. Claude Cristin, *Aux Origines de l'histoire littéraire* (Grenoble, 1973), pp. 28 - 49.

Chapter Two

1. Diego de Saavedra Fajardo, *Idea de un príncipe político-cristiano representada en cien empresas,* ed. Vicente Garcia de Diego, Clásicos Castellanos (Madrid, 1942), I, 8. Subsequent references in the text are to this edition.

2. Otis H. Green, "Documentos y datos sobre la estancia de Saavedra Fajardo en Italia," *Bulletin Hispanique* 39 (1937): 367 - 74.

3. Juan Torres Fontes, "Saavedra Fajardo en Roma y sus pretensiones a la canongía doctoral de Murcia," *Monteagudo,* No. 18 (1957), pp. 4 - 5.

4. Ibid., 6 - 11.

5. Diego de Saavedra Fajardo, "Epistolario," in *Obras completas,* ed. Angel González Palencia (Madrid, 1946), p. 1286. Subsequent references to the "Epistolario" are to this edition.

6. González Palencia, "Estudio preliminar" to Saavedra Fajardo, *Obras completas,* p. 20.

7. Juan Torres Fontes, "Saavedra Fajardo, chantre de la iglesia de Cartagena," *Monteagudo,* No. 16 (1956), pp. 20 - 26. Juan de Saavedra did not reside in Cartagena either, but his father took possession of the post. The son received first a one year's dispensation, and then because he was very young, he was allowed another five years to finish his studies.

8. Green, "Documentos. . . ."

9. José Raneo, *Libro donde se trata de los vireyes lugartenientes del reino de Nápoles y de las cosas tocantes a su grandeza compilado por José Raneo, año MDCXXXIV,* ed. Eustaquio Fernández de Navarrete, CODOIN, V. 23 (Madrid, 1853), 407.

10. British Museum, Egerton MS. 338, fols. 136v - 138v. A partial translation is to be found in Martin A. S. Hume, *The Court of Philip IV: Spain in Decadence* (New York/London, 1907), pp. 50 - 52. I have preferred my own version directly from the manuscript.

11. Archivo Histórico de Protocolos, Prot. 2712 (Bartolomé Gallo, 1632), fols. 1 - 88. Consult Cristóbal Pérez Pastor, *Bibliografía madrileña* (Madrid, 1891 - 1907), III, 353, 461, 465.

12. Gutierre Marqués de Careaga, *Desengaño de fortuna* (Barcelona, 1611), B. N. M., call number, R/8233; (Madrid, 1612), B. N. M., R/7155.

13. Nicolás Antonio, *Bibliotheca Hispana Nova* (Madrid, 1788), I, 561.

14. *Poesías diversas compuestas en diferentes lenguas en las honras que hizo en Roma la Nación de los Españoles. A la Majestad Católica de la Reina Doña Margarita de Austria, Nuestra Señora* (Roma, 1611), 56 fols.

15. *República literaria*, ed. García de Diego, pp. 60 - 62.

16. *Cigarrales de Toledo*, ed. Víctor Said Armesto (Madrid, 1913), p. 327. For the question of attribution, see the following: Adolfo de Castro, ed., *Poetas líricos de los siglos XVI y XVII*, B. A. E., 42 (Madrid, 1951), II, 157. José María Cossío, "El soneto 'A una fuente', atribuido a Saavedra Fajardo," *Correo Erudito* 2 (1941): 108 - 10. Juan Manuel Rozas, "Los textos dispersos de Villamediana," *Revista de Filología Española* 47 (1964): 341 - 67, especially 363 - 67.

17. Baltasar Gracián, *Agudeza y arte de ingenio*, Discurso XIII, in *Obras completas*, 3rd ed., ed. Arturo del Hoyo (Madrid, 1967), pp. 293 - 94.

18. José María Cossío, *Los toros en la poesía castellana* (Madrid, 1931), I, 167 - 73. A facsimile edition of the *Anfiteatro de Felipe el Grande* was published by Antonio Pérez Gómez (Cieza, 1974). Saavedra's poem is on fol. 71v - 72r.

19. Alfonso Reyes, "Ruiz de Alarcón y las fiestas de Baltasar Carlos," in *Capítulos de literatura española*, 1a serie (México, 1939), p. 221.

20. The title, *In Ictu Oculi*, is from I Corinthians, XV, 52. In the context of the chapter it does not seem appropriate for the subject matter of Valdés Leal's painting, for St. Paul is writing of the Resurrection at the Last Judgment. The Vulgate, XV, 51 - 52, reads: "Ecce mysterium vobis dico: Omnes quidem resurgemus, sed non omnes immutabimur. In momento, in ictu oculi, in novissima tuba: canet enim tuba, et mortui resurgent incorrupti et nos immutabimur." The *New English Bible* reads: "Listen! I will unfold a mystery: we shall not all die, but we shall all be changed in a flash, in the twinkling of an eye, at the last trumpet-call. For the trumpet will sound, and the dead will rise immortal, and we shall be changed."

21. Giorgio Spini, "Uno scritto sconsciuto di Saavedra Fajardo," *Hispania: Revista Española de Historia* 8 (1942): 438 - 51. I believe, on the basis of the external and internal evidence that Spini adduces, we may reasonably accept this tract, at least tentatively, as belonging to Saavedra.

22. Diego de Saavedra Fajardo, *Introducciones a la política, y Razón de estado del Rey Católico Don Fernando*, in *Obras*, B. A. E., 25 (reprint, Madrid, 1947), p . 423.

23. Juan de Mariana, *The King and His Education*, translated by George A. Moore (Washington, D. C., 1948), 440 pp.

24. The *"Fortuna" of Manuel de Faria e Sousa: An Autobiography*, introduction, edition, notes, and index by Edward Glaser (Münster, Westfalen: Aschendorffsche Verlagsbuchhandlung, 1975), p. 82. Subsequent citations are given in the text.

25. The document has been published by Quintín Aldea, "España, el Papado y el Imperio durante la Guerra de los Treinta Años. I. Instrucciones a los Embajadores de España en Roma (1631 - 1643)," *Miscelánea Comillas* 29 (1958): 303.

26. Ibid., p. 306.

27. J. H. Whitfield, *Machiavelli* (Oxford, 1947), p. 13.

28. Niccolò Machiavelli, *The Prince and The Discourses*, trans., Luigi Ricci and E. R. P. Vincent, introduction by Max Lerner (New York: Random House, 1940), p. 65.

29. Pedro de Ribadeneyra, *Tratado de la religión y virtudes que debe tener el príncipe cristiano para gobernar y conservar sus estados, contra lo que Nicolás Maquiavelo y los políticos deste tiempo enseñan* (Short title: *Tratado del príncipe cristiano*), in *Obras escogidas*, ed. Vincente de la Fuente, B. A. E., 60 (Madrid, 1868), p. 520.

30. Saavedra Fajardo, "Epistolario," in *Obras completas*, ed. González Palencia, p. 1290.

31. Heinrich Günter, *Die Habsburger Liga, 1625 - 1635: Briefe und Akten aus dem General-Archiv zu Simancas* (Berlin, 1908), pp. 256 - 58.

32. Alfred van der Essen, *Le Cardinal-Enfant et la politique européene de l'Espagne, 1609 - 1641* (Brussels, 1944), I, 161, n. 4.

33. Saavedra Fajardo, "Epistolario" in *Obras completas*, ed. González Palencia, pp. 1303 - 04.

34. van der Essen, *Le Cardinal-Enfant . . .* , pp. 140 - 42, 150, 287 - 88.

35. Ibid., p. 426.

36. González Palencia, "Estudio preliminar" to Saavedra Fajardo, *Obras completas*, pp. 47, 52.

37. van der Essen, *Le Cardinal-Enfant . . .* , p. 371.

38. Cited by José María Jover, *1635: Historia de una polémica y semblanza de una generación* (Madrid, 1949), p. 64.

39. I have not seen a French version. The citation is from the Spanish version reprinted by Jover, *1635: Historia de una polémica. . .* , p. 475.

40. Jover, *1635: Historia de una polémica . . .* , pp. 512 - 24, reproduces, in part, the printed text, a copy of which is to be found in B. N. M., MS. 2366 beginning at fol. 345.

41. Jover, *1635: Historia de una polémica . . .* , p. 513.

42. Manuel Fraga Iribane, *Don Diego de Saavedra y Fajardo y la diplomacia de su época* (Madrid, 1955), p. 243.

43. For the text see Saavedra Fajardo, *Sus pensamientos, sus poesías, sus opúsculos*, ed. Conde de Roche and José Pío Tejera, pp. 179 - 90; and *Obras completas*, ed. A. González Palencia, pp. 1323 - 28. Citations in the text are to the latter edition.

44. The *Dispertador* is in Saavedra Fajardo, *Sus pensamientos, sus poesías, sus opúsculos*, ed. Conde de Roche and José Pío Tejera, pp. 217 - 28. The B. N. M. MS is described on pp. 155 and 219. The document may also be read in *Obras completas*, ed. Angel González Palencia, pp. 1329 - 33. My citations are from the latter text.

45. I use the short title. The full title is: *Relación de Don Diego de Saavedra Fajardo, consejero del Supremo y Real Consejo de Indias, Embajador por Su Magestad Católica del rey Don Phelipe Cuarto el Grande N.*

Señor al Elector de Baviera, de la jornada que por orden de Su Magestad hizo el año de mil seiscientos y treinta y ocho al condado de Borgoña. It is printed in Saavedra Fajardo, *Sus pensamientos, sus poesías, sus opúsculos,* ed. Conde de Roche and José Pío Tejera, pp. 152 - 67; and in *Obras completas,* ed. González Palencia, pp. 1333 - 41. I cite from the latter text.

46. Saavedra's words are "mozo de ingenio turbado" (*Obras completas,* p. 1335). Lisola must have been even then simply a patriot of his county of Burgundy. As a result of the events of 1638, he went to Vienna where the imperial government recognized his potential talents and gave him a job. Thus, he began a diplomatic career in the service of the Empire and became an implacable adversary of Louis XIV and France. His story is told by Emile Longin, *Un Diplomate franc-comtois, François de Lisola: sa vie, ses écrits, son testament (1613 - 1674),* (Dôle, 1900).

47. Luis Quer y Boule, *La embajada de Saavedra Fajardo en Suiza: apuntes históricos, 1639 - 1642* (Madrid, 1931), pp. 53 - 54.

48. *Obras completas,* ed. González Palencia, p. 1353.

49. Quintín Aldea, "Don Diego Saavedra Fajardo y la paz de Europa: dos documentos inéditos, en el tercer centenario de la Paz de los Pirineos, 1659 - 1959," *Humanidades* (Universidad Pontificia de Comillas) 9, No. 22 (1956): 105.

50. Luis Quer y Boule, *Aspuntes hispano suizos* (Madrid, 1931), pp. 89 - 90.

Chapter Three

1. Horace, *Satires, Epistles and Ars Poetica,* trans. H. Rushton Fairclough, Loeb Classical Library, 194 (Cambridge, Mass., 1966), pp. 478 - 79 (*Ars Poetica,* vv. 343 - 44).

2. The seventeenth-century contribution to this vast literature has been studied by José Antonio Maravall, *La teoría española del estado en el siglo XVII* (Madrid, 1944), 428 pp.

3. Sebastián de Covarrubias y Orozco, *Tesoro de la lengua castellana o española,* ed. Martín de Riquer (Barcelona, 1943), p. 506.

4. Quoted by Maravall, pp. 45 - 49.

5. José Sánchez, "Nombres que reemplazan a *capítulo* en libros antiguos," *Hispanic Review* 11 (1945): 143 - 61. Otis H. Green, "On the Meaning of *Crisi(s)* before *El critic.in,*" *Hispanic Review* 21 (1953): 218 - 20.

6. The references to *The Royal Politician* are to the Clásicos Castellanos edition of *Idea de un príncipe político-cristiano representada en cien empreses,* ed. Vicente García de Diego (Madrid, 1942 - 46), 4 vols.

7. "Aprobación" to Francisco Garau, *El sabio instruido de la naturaleza* (Madrid, 1677), unnumbered.

8. Diego de Saavedra Fajardo, *Corona gótica, castellana y austriaca,* in *Obras completas,* ed. Angel González Palencia (Madrid, 1946), p. 706.

9. There were one hundred essays in the first edition, as the title says. However, Saavedra made several changes in the Milan edition (dated 1642)

with the result that there are 101 essays in it, but he did not change the title. Because the changes were made by Saavedra himself, the Milan edition is considered the authoritative one, and the B. A. E., Clásicos Castellanos, and Aguilar editions are based on it. For an explanation of the changes see García de Diego, "Prólogo" to *Idea de un príncipe*, I, lii - lv.

10. Marcelino Menéndez y Pelayo, *Historia de las ideas estéticas en España* (Madrid, 1896), III, 398.

11. José María Jover, *1635; Historia de una polémica y semblanza de una generación* (Madrid, 1949), pp. 296 - 98.

12. Martin Esslin, *Brecht: The Man and His Work*, rev. ed. (Garden City, N. Y., 1971), pp. 310 - 11.

13. Javier Márquez, "El mercantilismo de Saavedra Fajardo," *El Trimestre Económico* 10 (1943): 268, note 23.

14. Juan de Mariana, *The King and His Education*, trans. George Albert Moore (Washington, D. C., 1948), p. 209. The subject of Tacitism has been studied by Enrique Tierno Galván in "El tacitismo en las doctrinas del Siglo de Oro," *Anales de la Universidad de Murcia* (1949), 895 - 988; and by José Antonio Maravall in "La corriente doctrinal del tacitismo político en España," *Cuadernos Hispanoamericanos*, Nos. 238 - 240 (1969), pp. 645 - 67.

15. *República literaria*, p. 120. Budé, also called Budaeus (1468 - 1540), a French scholar, was a friend of Erasmus.

16. García de Diego, "Prólogo" to *Idea de un príncipe*, I, xxix - xxxii.

17. Juan Huarte de San Juan, *Examen de ingenios* in *Obras de filósofos*, ed. Adolfo de Castro, B. A. E., 65 (Madrid, 1873), p. 405.

18. Baltasar Gracián, *El héroe y El discreto*, ed. Arturo Farinelli (Madrid, 1900), pp. 9 - 10, 19.

19. Mariana, *The King and His Education*, p. 343.

20. Covarrubias, *Tesoro de la lengua castellana*, II, fol. 150.

21. *Diccionario de le lengua castellana* (Madrid, 1726 - 39), V, 418.

22. Margaret J. Bates, *"Discreción" in the Works of Cervantes: A Semantic Study* (Washington, D. C., 1945), pp. 14, 59 - 64, 66 - 73.

23. Niccoló Machiavelli, *The Prince*, trans., Luigi Ricci and E. R. P. Vincent, and *The Discourses*, trans. by Christian E. Detmold; intro. by Max Lerner (New York, 1940), p. 64. This and subsequent passages are quoted by permission of the Oxford University Press.

24. Pedro de Rivadeneira, *Tratado del príncipe cristiano*, in *Obras escogidas*, ed. Vincente de la Fuente, B. A. E., 60 (Madrid, 1868), p. 552.

25. *Epistolario*, in *Obras completas*, ed. Angel González Palencia (Madrid, 1946), p. 1328.

26. St. Thomas Aquinas, *On the Governance of Rulers*, trans. Gerald B. Phelan (New York, 1938), p. 52.

27. Luis de Granada, *Guía de pecadores*, ed. Matías Martínez Burgos (Madrid, 1929), p. 197. The problem is weighed by Monroe Z. Hafter, "Deviousness in Saavedra Fajardo's *Idea de un príncipe*," *The Romanic Review* 49 (1958): 161 - 67.

28. Gracián, *El héroe*, pp. 7 - 8. The problem of the Spanish moralists is excellently presented by Donald W. Bleznick, "Spanish Reaction to Machiavelli in the Sixteenth and Seventeenth Centuries," *Journal of the History of Ideas* 19 (1958): 542 - 50.

29. Machiavelli, *The Prince*, p. 65.

30. Gracián, *El héroe*, p. 47. The subject is treated extensively by Monroe Z. Hafter in *Gracián and Perfection: Spanish Moralists of the Seventeenth Century* (Cambridge, Mass., 1966).

31. Rivadeneira, *Tratado del príncipe cristiano*, p. 526.

32. Machiavelli, *Discourses*, pp. 284 - 85.

33. Rivadeneira, *Tratado del príncipe cristiano*, p. 573 ff.

34. Cristóbal Suárez de Figueroa, *Hechos de Don García Hurtado de Mendoza, cuarto marqués de Cañete*, ed. Diego Barros Arana, in Colección de Historiadores de Chile y Documentos Relativos a la Historia Nacional, 5 (Santiago de Chile, 1864), pp. 1 - 2.

35. The Granadan poet Pedro Soto de Rojas (1588? - 1658) belonged to Saavedra's generation, and one of his books was entitled *Paraíso cerrado para muchos, jardines abiertos para pocos* (Granada, 1652).

36. Carmelo M. Bonet, "En torno al estilo de Saavedra Fajardo," *Boletín de la Academia Argentina de Letras* 9 (1941): 121 - 33.

37. Mayáns first published the *Oración en alabanza de las obras de Don Diego Saavedra Fajardo* in 1725 (see Bibliography). I quote from the text which he later included in his edition of *República literaria* (Madrid, 1735), p. xi.

38. Benito Jerónimo Feijoo, *Cartas eruditas*, ed. Agustín Millares Carlo (Madrid, 1958), pp. 22 - 23.

39. José de Cadalso, *Cartas marruecas*, ed. Lucien Dupuis and Nigel Glendinning (London, 1966), p. 33.

40. José Luis Munárriz, *Lecciones sobre la retórica y las bellas artes por Hugo Blair* (Madrid, 1798 - 1801), II, 211. Subsequent citations in the text are to this edition.

41. Ramón de Mesonero Romanos, "El romanticismo y los románticos," in *Escenas matritenses*, ed. Federico Carlos de Robles (Madrid, 1956), p. 607.

42. José Martínez Ruiz [Azorín], "Saavedra Fajardo," *Obras completas* (Madrid, 1947 - 54), 313 - 40.

Chapter Four

1. Antoine Brun was attorney general *(procureur général)* of the Parlement of Dôle when Saavedra was in Franche-Comté in 1638. Later he served with Saavedra at the Congress of Westphalia in Münster. See Emile Longin, *Un diplomate franc-comtois: François de Lisola, sa vie, ses écrits, son testament, 1613 - 1674* (Dôle, 1900), p. 6, note 4.

2. Fraga Iribarne, *Don Diego de Saavedra y Fajardo y la diplomacia de su época*, (Madrid, 1955), pp. 355 - 56. On the first edition of *Idea de un príncipe* see A. Huarte, "La edición príncipe de las *Empresas políticas* de

Saavedra Fajardo," *Revista de la Biblioteca, Archivo y Museo del Ayuntamiento de Madrid* 10 (1933): 91 - 97.

3. There is an excellent critical edition of this work: Francisco de Quevedo Villegas, *Política de Dios. Govierno de Christo*, ed. James O. Crosby (Madrid, 1966), 604 pp.

4. Fraga Iribarne, *Don Diego de Saavedra y Fajardo y la diplomacia de su época*, pp. 379 - 95.

5. *Obras completas*, ed. González Palencia, pp. 1352 - 54.

6. The text has been printed from British Library MS. Addison 14,000, fols. 524 - 535v, by Quintín Aldea, "Don Diego Saavedra Fajardo y la paz de Europa . . . ," *Humanidades* 9 (1956): 103 - 124, from which I cite. The attribution is established by Saavedra himself in a letter to Philip IV dated May 6, 1644 (*Obras completas*, ed. González Palencia, p. 1383).

7. G. J. Bougeant, *Histoire de la Paix de Westphalie* (Paris, 1751), II, 303.

8. An excellent English edition which contains the *Formulae* is now available: *The Colloquies of Erasmus*, tr. Craig R. Thompson (Chicago and London, 1965).

9. Adapted from the 1727 London ed., pp. 122 - 23. Marcel Bataillon calls attention to the passage in *Erasmo y España* (Mexico, 1950), II, 398, note 18.

10. Alfonso de Valdés, *Diálogo de las cosas ocurridas en Roma* [ed. J. F. Montesinos] (Madrid, 1946), p. 3. I have only suggested certain antecedents. The rich dialogue literature of Spain in the sixteenth century also includes such works as the translation of Castiglione's *El cortesano* (1528), León Hebreo's *Diálogos de amor* (1535), Pedro Mexía's *Diálogos o coloquios* (1547), Antonio de Torquemada's *Coloquios satíricos* (1553), Cristóbal de Villalón's *El viaje de Turquía* (1553), Lorenzo Suárez de Chaves's *Diálogos de varias cuestiones* (1577), and Luis de León's *De los nombres de Cristo* (1585).

11. The significance of the dialogue genre in France, and hence in Europe, during the very period in which Saavedra published *Locuras de Europa* is demonstrated by Phillip J. Wolfe, "Dialogue et société: Le genre du dialogue en France de 1630 á 1671" (Ph.D. diss., Princeton, 1974).

12. I cite from the text in *Obras completas*, ed. Angel González Palencia (Madrid, 1946), beginning with p. 1198. Subsequent page numbers are given in the text.

13. Vicente Salvá, *A Catalogue of Spanish and Portuguese Books, with Occasional Literary and Bibliographical Remarks* (London: M. Calero, 1926), item 1899, p. 187.

14. Saavedra Fajardo, *Corona gótica* in *Obras completas*, ed. González Palencia, pp. 708 - 09. This text is based on the first edition of 1646 with spelling modernized. Subsequent references in the text are to it.

15. González Palencia, "Estudio preliminar" to Saavedra Fajardo, *Obras completas*, p. 121.

16. González Palencia lists these moral reflections, pp. 696 - 97.

17. His words are cast in a typically Baroque way: "el oficio de historiador no es de enseñar refiriendo, sino de referir enseñando" (*Corona gótica*, p. 706).

18. Luis Cabrera de Córdoba, *De historia para entenderla y escribirla* (Madrid, 1611), fol. 19.

19. Ramón Menéndez Pidal, *El Rey Rodrigo en la literatura* (Madrid, 1924), pp. 146 - 47.

20. Notes are omitted in the B. A. E. edition, v. 25; but González Palencia includes them in the *Obras completas*.

21. Nicolás Antonio, *Bibliotheca Hispana Nova* (Madrid, 1783 - 88), I, 38 - 39.

22. A single letter appeared in *Continuación de los documentos relativos a Don Pedro Girón, Tercer Duque de Osuna*, CODOIN, 47 (Madrid, 1865), 476. There are eighty-four letters and notes in José Sancho Rayón and Francisco de Zabalburu, *Correspondencia diplomática de los plenipotenciarios españoles en el Congreso de Münster, 1643 a 1648*, CODOIN, 82 (Madrid, 1884), 3 - 62, 501 - 57.

23. Duquesa de Berwick y de Alba, *Documentos escogidos del archivo de la casa de Alba* (Madrid, 1891), p. 471.

24. Fraga Iribarne, *Don Diego de Saavedra y Fajardo y la diplomacia de su época*, pp. 655 - 70.

25. It is reproduced in Jover, *1635: Historia de una polémica. . .* , facing p. 460. Terborch did a second painting, *Delegates Swearing to the Peace Treaty*, now in London. It is reproduced in Frank Jewett Mather, Jr., *Western European Painting of the Renaissance* (New York, 1948), Fig. 296, p. 534. Both paintings are dated 1648. I cannot be certain that Saavedra himself appears in either painting. He returned to Madrid in 1646, the same year that Terborch arrived in Münster.

26. Professor Monroe Z. Hafter called my attention to the "Aprobación" of this book published in Madrid by Francisco García in 1648.

27. [Mariano Roca de Togores, Marqués de Molíns], "Historia de la calavera de un grande hombre," *Semanario Pintoresco Español* I (1836): 55. By the same author, "Noticias sobre la traslacíon de los restos de D. Diego Saavedra Fajardo a la ciudad de Murcia," in Roche and Tejera, *Saavedra Fajardo: sus pensamientos, sus poesías, sus opúsculos*, pp. clx - clxxx. To be sure, Roca de Togores's statements must be accepted with caution as Carmen de Burgos showed in her biography of Larra, *Fígaro* (Madrid, 1919), passim.

28. González Palencia, "Estudio preliminar" to *Obras completas*, p. 131.

29. Javier Fuentes y Ponte, *Sumario del descubrimiento de los restos de Saavedra Fajardo* (Murcia, 1883), 13 pp.

Selected Bibliography

PRIMARY SOURCES

Given are the first edition of Saavedra's works and significant subsequent editions, plus important collected works. Because of the rarity of the sources, and the existence of variants, the primary bibliography is annotated, despite TWAS practice to the contrary.

1. *Manuscripts*
Manuscripts of several minor works have survived, but I list only the two highly important ones of *República literaria.*
B. N. M. MS. 6436. "Republica Literaria. / Por Don Diego Saavedra Faxardo / Caballero de la orden / de Santiago / Del Consejo de Su Magd en / el Supremo de las Indias." In another hand: "año de 1612." 98 fols. Handwriting of the seventeenth century with autograph corrections and additions. This is the "long" text of *República literaria* and is today considered the most authentic version.
B. N. M. MS. 7526. "República literaria" in "Mamotreto / o / índice para la memoria / y vso de / Don Jvan Vélez de León / qve se difinió a sí mesmo / en este / soneto." This miscellany begins with the aforementioned sonnet and contains many items, among them the "short" text of *República literaria.* The collection consists of 262 fols. without continuous numbering. The folios containing the *República literaria* are numbered 620 - 33, a fact that suggests that they came from a different collection. The handwriting is of the seventeenth century. There is no title page, but a note on a small piece of paper, written in a different hand of either the seventeenth or eighteenth century, says: "This is the *República literaria* as it first left the pen and mind of Don Diego de Saavedra. . . ."

2. *Individual Works* (in chronological order)

República literaria

Juicio de artes y ciencias. Su autor Don Claudio Antonio de Cabrera. Sácale a la común censura D. Melchor de Fonseca y Almeida. Madrid: Julián Paredes, 1655, [26[+ 95 ff. This is the first printed edition of the long text of the *República literaria.* It did not bear Saavedra's

name. The assumption is that Cabrera is a pseudonym made up by
Fonseca.

República literaria. Escribióla D. Diego de Saavedra Fajardo, Caballero de
la Orden de Santiago, del Consejo de su Magestad en el Supremo de
Indias, y su Plenipotenciario para la Paz Universal. Alcalá de
Henares: María Fernandez, 1670, [60] + 159 pp. The first printed
edition with the title *República literaria* and Saavedra's name was
published by José de Salinas and Francisco Ignacio de Porres. The
latter wrote a prologue which, though stylistically poor, is important
for the history of the work. This text was the basis for subsequent
editions, which then deviated from it.

República literaria. Bruselas: Lamberto Marchant, 1677. This edition is
significant because it was printed from a copy of the 1670 Alcalá text
from which the last page was missing. Thus, the Brussels and
Antwerp editions, as well as translations based on them, present a
variant conclusion.

República literaria. [Ed. Gregorio Mayáns y Siscar]. Valencia: Antonio
Balle, 1730. Mayáns wrote a critical judgment and note to the reader
that is different from his *Oración* of 1725 (see "Works by Other
Authors" below), and he also revised the text in accordance with
criteria that modern scholarship finds unacceptable.

República literaria. Obra póstuma de Don Diego Saavedra Fajardo.
Madrid: Juan de Zúñiga, 1735, xliv + 110 † xxiv pp. In the second
edition of Mayáns' text, he presents a preface different from the
critical judgment and note of the 1730 edition and reproduces the
Oración of 1725.

República literaria. [Ed. Francisco García Prieto]. Madrid: Benito Cano,
1788. This handsomely printed edition, with engravings, reproduces
the Mayáns text. There are thirty-five notes, presumably by the
editor; and the "Noticias pertenecientes a Don Diego Saavedra Fajardo," by José de Guevara y Vasconcelos are an important early
study ranking with the Porres "Prólogo" and the Mayáns *Oración*.

Modern Editions

República literaria. Ed. Vicente García de Diego. Clásicos Castellanos, 46.
Madrid: Ediciones de "La Lectura," 1922. This is the first printed
text based on B. N. M. MS. 6436. Calling it the "texto anterior,"
García de Diego prints in footnotes the "primitive text" that Serrano
y Sanz published in 1907. He also gives variants from the 1788 ed.
(based on Mayáns), a 1790 ed. (based on the 1670 Alcalá ed.), and
the B. A. E. text (also based on Mayáns). There is a reprint of 1942
with the pages renumbered but without substantive changes.

República literaria. Ed. Vicente García de Diego. Clásicos Castellanos, 46.
2nd ed. Madrid: Espasa-Calpe, 1956. The significant difference
between this second edition and that of 1922 is the inclusion of
variants directly from the 1670 Alcalá text. A few notes to the in-

troduction have been revised in order to take into account recent
scholarship.

República literaria. Ed. John Dowling. Salamanca, Madrid, Barcelona,
Caracas: Anaya, 1967. The text is based on B. N. M. MS. 6436 with
modernized orthography. It follows, with slight variation, the
divisions used in the 1788 Madrid edition.

English Translations

*The Commonwealth of Learning, or A Censure on Learned Men and
Sciences.* London: J. Nutt, 1705. The translator's name is not given.
The text is based on one of the Brussels/Antwerp editions with the
shortened final sentence.

Respublica Literaria, or The Republick of Letters, Being a Vision. [Trans. J.
E.] London: S. Austen, 1727. The translation is also based on the
Brussels/Antwerp text with the final shortened sentence. The
translator confesses to making omissions. This text was reprinted the
next year: London and Dublin: Samuel Fuller, 1728.

"Short" Text

*Discurso curioso, agudo y erudito acerca de la multitud de libros que cada
día se publican, y juicio de los autores en todas facultades, así modernos como antiguos.* Escribióle en meditación retirada, nacida de la
continua lición y estudio de todo género de escritores, N. de N.,
Secretario de S. M. In *Gabinete de Lectura Española* VI. Madrid:
Imprenta de Sancha, [1794]. This is the first printed version of the
"short" text of *República literaria.* It was based on a MS in the
library of the Reales Estudios de San Isidro that has been lost but
which may be B. N. M. MS. 7526, which has no proper title page.
The editor of the *Gabinete* was Isidoro Bosarte; the author of the
prologue was Pedro Estala.

*El texto primitivo de la República literaria de Don Diego de Saavedra y
Fajardo.* Ed. M. Serrano y Sanz. Madrid: Imprenta Ibérica a cargo de
T. Maestre, 1907. Serrano published the "short" text of B. N. M. MS.
7526.

Idea de un príncipe

*Idea de un príncipe político christiano. Representada en cien empresas.
Dedicada al Príncipe de las Españas Nuestro Señor por Don Diego
Saavedra Fajardo del Consejo de su Magestad en el Supremo de las
Indias, i su Embajador extraordinario en Mantua i Esguízaros i
Residente en Alemania.* Mónaco: Nicolao Enrico, 1640. First edition,
published in Munich, Germany. For the description I rely on García
de Diego's Clásicos Castellanos edition (I, li). It contains one hun-
dred essays besides the prologue and the final poem.

*Idea de vn príncipe político christiano. Rapresentada [sic] en cien empresas.
Dedicada al Príncipe de las Españas Nvestro Señor por Don Diego de
Saauedra Faxardo, Cauallero del Orden de S. Iago, del Consejo de su*

Magd. en el Supremo de las Indias, i su Embajador Plenipotenciario en los Treze Cantones, en la Dieta Imperial de Ratisbona por el Circulo i Casa de Borgoña, i en el Congreso de Munster para la Paz General. Mónaco, 1640; Milán, 1642. The second edition, which lacked the name of a publisher, appeared after the date of the title page, for it contains material dated as late as October 6, 1643. Saavedra revised the text, and there are now 101 essays, although he did not change the title page. This text has served as the basis for subsequent editions. García de Diego in the prologue to the Clásicos Castellanos edition (II, liii - lv) describes the revisions.

Idea de un príncipe político cristiano representada en cien empresas. Ed. Vicente García de Diego. 4 vols. Clásicos Castellanos, 76, 81, 87, 102. Madrid: Ediciones de "La Lectura," 1927 - 30. This is an accessible and reliable modern edition.

English Translation

The Royal Politician Represented in One Hundred Emblems. Translated by James Astry. 2 vols. London: M. Gylliflower and L. Meredith, 1700.

Corona gótica

Corona gothica, castellana y austriaca, políticamente ilustrada. Parte primera. Dedicada al príncipe de las Españas, Nuestro Señor. Por don Diego Saavedra Faxardo, cavallero de la Orden de Santiago, del Consejo de su Magestad en el Supremo de las Indias, y su Plenipotenciario para la paz vniversal. Münster: Juan Jansonio, 1646. This first edition contains only the history of the Gothic kings of Spain.

Corona gothica, castellana, y avstriaca, políticamente ilustrada. Por Don Diego Saavedra Faxardo . . . . 3 vols. Madrid: Andrés García de la Iglesia, 1670 - 77. The title page of v. 2 says: "Segvnda parte, compvesta de algvnos originales que quedaron de D. Diego de Saauedra Faxardo, y continuada por D. Alonso Núñez de Castro, Coronista [sic] de Su Magestad." Those parts of the *Corona castellana* that are by Saavedra may be read in *Obras completas,* ed. González Palencia, pp. 1069 - 1124.

Locuras de Europa

Locuras de Europa. Diálogo pósthumo de Don Diego Saavedra Fajardo. . . . N. P., 1748. It is thought that this edition, the first known printed text, appeared in Germany.

Locuras de Europa. Diálogo entre Mercurio y Luciano, por Don Diego de Saavedra del Consejo de Su Magestad en el de Indias. Ed. Antonio Valladares de Sotomayor. In *Semanario Erudito* 6 (1787), 3 - 44. The editor, unacquainted with the 1748 edition, believed he was printing this work for the first time.

Locuras de Europa. Ed. José M. Alejandro. Salamanca, Madrid, Barcelona: Anaya, [1965]. The editor used the B. A. E. text, which in turn was based on that of Valladares in *Semanario Erudito.*

3. *Other Tracts and Essays* (in chronological order)

Indisposizione generale della monarchia di Spagna. This tract, written in Italian and dated 1630, was included in a work printed in 1646 at Genoa (but falsely said to be at Lyons) and was attributed to a Spanish diplomat. Giorgio Spini in "Uno scritto sconosciuto di Saavedra" (see Secondary Sources below) explains the bibliographical history, reprints it, and argues for Saavedra's authorship.

Introducciones a la política, y Razón de estado de Rey Católico Don Fernando. In *Obras,* B. A. E. 25, 423 - 42; and in *Obras completas,* ed. González Palencia, 1224 - 56. Dated 1631, these two titles were conceived as first and second parts of a single work. Saavedra left them unfinished, and they were first published in 1853 in the B. A. E. from B. N. M.MS. 1165. (Another manuscript is numbered 10838.)

Respuesta al manifesto de Francia. Madrid: Francisco Martínez, 1635. 30 fols. The only known copy of this anonymous pamphlet is to be found in B. N. M. MS. 2366, fols. 345 1 - 30. It is partially reproduced in Jover, *1635: Historia de una polémica y semblanza de una generación,* pp. 512 - 24.

Discurso de Don Diego de Saavedra Fajardo sobre el estado presente de Europa. This essay (1637), intended for the Cardinal-Infante Fernando and the Count-Duke of Olivares, is preserved in B. N. M. MSS. 18630, No. 36, and 18653, No. 10. It was transcribed by Roche and Tejera, *Saavedra Fajardo: Sus pensamientos . . . ,* pp. 177 - 90, and was reprinted in *Obras completas,* ed. González Palencia, pp. 1323 - 28.

Dispertador a los trece cantones de esquízaros. This propaganda tract, preserved in B. N. M. MS. 2369, "Sucesos del año de 1638," was printed by Roche and Tejera, *Saavedra Fajardo: sus pensamientos . . . ,* pp. 217 - 28, and reprinted in *Obras completas,* ed. González Palencia, pp. 1329 - 33.

Relación de la jornada al condado de Borgoña. Saavedra reports to Philip IV on the results of his mission to the crown province of Franche-Comté in 1638. Preserved in B. N. M. MS. 2369, "Sucesos del año de 1638," it was printed by Roche and Tejera, *Saavedra Fajardo: sus pensamientos . . . ,* pp. 152 - 76, and reprinted in *Obras completas,* ed. González Palencia, pp. 1333 - 41.

Relation du voyage de Saavedra Fajardo au Comté de Bourgogne, 1638. Edited and translated by Emile Longin. Besançon: Marion, 1923. The translator provides an introduction and notes to Saavedra's report.

Proposta fatta dal Sig. Don Diego Sciavedra alla Dieta de cantoni catolici in Lucerna. This document, written in Italian and dated 1639, was a part of Saavedra's continuing propaganda effort to maintain the

neutrality of the Swiss. It is known from a Vatican Library MS which
Quintín Aldea printed in his article, "Don Diego Saavedra Fajardo y
la paz de Europa. . . ." (See Secondary Sources below.)
Suspiros de Francia. Quintín Aldea printed this short tract, written in 1643,
from British Library MS. Addison 14,000, fols. 524 - 535v, in his article "Don Diego Saavedra Fajardo y la paz de Europa. . . ." (see
below).

4. *Correspondence*
*Correspondencia diplomática de los plenipotenciarios españoles en el
Congreso de Münster, 1643 a 1648.* In CODOIN, v. 82. Madrid: Im-
prenta de Miguel Ginesta, 1884. This first collection of Saavedra's
letters appeared in the same year as Roche and Tejera's *Saavedra
Fajardo: sus pensamientos.* . . . The two works mark the point of
departure for modern scholarly studies of his life and works.
Epistolario. In *Obras completas,* ed. González Palencia, pp. 1281 - 1437.
The editor collected all letters that were known to him at the time
the volume appeared. He gives 119 items, including those in
CODOIN, v. 82, and other scattered sources. Some of the items I
have included among Saavedra's tracts and essays.
Note: Fraga Iribarne (see below) in *Don Diego de Saavedra y Fajardo y
la diplomacia de su época* transcribes or translates, in footnotes and either
in part or in full, a great many letters by Saavedra. It is evident that the correspondence of Saavedra requires a new edition.

5. *Undiscovered Works*
In letters to Philip IV dated May 3, and May 6, 1644 (*Obras completas,*
ed. González Palencia, pp. 1380, 1383), Saavedra mentions the following
works which have not been discovered:
Carta de un holandés a otro ministro de aquellos estados (a tract which he
printed after 1638).
Guerras y movimientos de Italia, de cuarenta años a esta parte (a book that
he had ready for the press in 1644).
Carta de un francés a otro del Parlamento de París (a tract which he printed
in Frankfort in 1643 or 1644).
Tratados de ligas y confederaciones de Francia con holandeses y sueceses (a
tract which he sent to Brussels to be printed in 1643 or 1644).

6. *Collected Works*
Obras. 3 or 4 vols. Antwerp: Juan Bautista Verdussen, 1677 - 1739. Handsome individual editions of *Idea de un príncipe, República literaria,*
and *Corona gótica, castellana y austriaca* (including the Núñez de
Castro continuation) were kept in print under different dates and
variously bound in three or four volumes under title pages which
were also renewed. A bibliographical study of these editions has not
been made.
Obras. B. A. E., 25. Madrid: M. Rivadeneyra, 1853. This was the first edi-

tion of collected works in one volume which aimed at being fairly complete. It was reprinted in 1861, 1866, 1926, and 1947. It has been supplanted by the González Palencia edition and superior editions of individual texts.

Saavedra Fajardo: sus pensamientos, sus poesías, sus opúsculos, precedidos de un discurso preliminar crítico, biográfico y bibliográfico sobre la vida y obras del autor e ilustrados con notas, introducciones y una genealogía de la casa de Saavedra. Eds. Conde de Roche and José Pío Tejera. Madrid: Imprenta de Fortanet, 1884. This volume has not been supplanted in usefulness despite the many studies that appeared after 1948, the tercentenary of Saavedra's death.

El pensamiento vivo de Saavedra Fajardo. Ed. Francisco Ayala. Buenos Aires: Editorial Losada, 1941. The title of this work and a lively introduction by a skillful writer did much to popularize Saavedra's writings in the Hispanic world. It appeared the year after the Spanish Cultural Institute in Buenos Aires celebrated the tercentenary of the publication of *Idea de un príncipe.*

Obras completas. Ed. Ángel González Palencia. Madrid: M. Aguilar, 1946. The extensive introduction, the inclusion of many brief works, and the collection of letters make this the most useful modern edition of Saavedra's works.

7. *Poetry*

CASCALES, FRANCISCO. *Tablas poéticas.* Murcia: Luis Beros, 1614. Among the laudatory poems at the beginning of the volume is the Latin epigram by Saavedra: "Hoc, bone lector, habes praecepta poetica libro. . . . " It is reproduced with a translation in *Saavedra Fajardo: sus pensamientos, sus poesías, sus opúsculos,* ed. Conde de Roche and José Pío Tejera, pp. 111 - 12; and in *Obras completas,* ed. González Palencia, p. 1269.

MARQUÉS DE CAREAGA, GUTIERRE. *Desengaño de fortuna.* Barcelona: Francisco Dotil, 1611. It seems ironical that this book was dedicated to Rodrigo Calderón, the powerful favorite of Philip III, who was executed in 1621 by order of the Count-Duke of Olivares. Saavedra Fajardo, with Juan Ruiz de Alarcón and others, was a contributor of poems in praise of Calderón and of the author. In the unnumbered preliminary folios there are two poems by Saavedra: one in Latin dedicated to Calderón, "Viribus Imperium Princeps generose quiescit . . ."; and one in Spanish directed to Marqués de Careaga, "Cantas con tal plectro y lira. . . . " Both may be read in *Obras completas,* ed. González Palencia, p. 1268. There is a second edition of the book: Madrid: Alonso Martín, 1612.

PELLICER Y TOVAR, JOSÉ, compiler. *Anfiteatro de Felipe el Grande.* Madrid: Juan González, 1631. Facsimile edition: Cieza: Antonio Pérez Gómez, 1974. Saavedra's two *espinelas* (ten-verse stanzas) about the bull that Philip IV killed begin "Hoy luze constelación / Aquel bizarro animal . . . ," fols. 71v - 72r.

Poesías diversas compuestas en diferentes lenguas en las honras que hizo en Roma la nación de los españoles a la Maxestad Católica de la Reyna doña Margarita de Austria Ntra. Señora. Roma: Jacomo Mascardo, 1612. Contains fourteen poems by Saavedra, three in Latin and eleven in Spanish, of which five are sonnets. One poem is directed to the Spanish ambassador in Rome, the Count of Castro, and the rest to Queen Margaret. All may be read in Roche and Tejera, *Sus pensamientos. . .* (with translations of the Latin), pp. 111 - 31; and in *Obras completas,* ed. González Palencia, pp. 1269 - 78.

Note: Only two other poems by Saavedra are known: (1) "Ludibria Mortis," which appeared at the end of *Idea de un príncipe* and which may be read in any edition of that work; (2) "A una fuente" (first verse: "Risa del monte, de las aves lira . . ."), which appeared in *República literaria.* His authorship of this poem is disputed.

8. *Works by Other Authors*

Included, along with other works of a different nature, is a selection of the most significant books of the sixteenth and seventeenth centuries which deal with politics and the education of princes.

FARIA E. SOUSA, MANUEL DE. *The "Fortuna" of Manuel de Faria e Sousa. An Autobiography.* Ed. Edward Glaser. Münster, Westfalen: Aschendorffsche Verlagsbuchhandlung, 1975. Professor Glaser publishes the autobiography of a Portuguese who knew Saavedra in Madrid and in Italy.

FERNÁNDEZ NAVARRETE, PEDRO. *Conservación de monarquías, y discursos políticos sobre la gran consulta que el consejo hizo al Señor Rey Don Felip III.* In *Obras,* B. A. E., 25, pp. 447 - 557. Madrid: M. Rivadeneyra, 1853. The author is concerned with the preservation of the state in the face of decline.

GRACIÁN, BALTASAR. *Obras completas,* 3rd ed. Ed. Arturo del Hoyo. Madrid: Aguilar, 1967. Besides *El político,* this edition contains other works by Gracián that are related in theme to Saavedra's books, especially *El héroe* and *El discreto.*

HUARTE DE SAN JUAN, JUAN. *Examen de ingenios.* Ed. Adolfo de Castro. In *Obras de filósofos,* B. A. E., 65, pp. 397 - 520. Madrid: M. Rivadeneyra, 1873. This early psychological treatise (1575) is fundamental for an understanding of Golden Age literature.

MARIANA, JUAN DE. *The King and His Education.* Translated by George A. Moore. Washington, D. C.: The Country Dollar Press, 1948. Mariana wrote his work in Latin: *De Rege et Regis Institutione.* A Spanish version is in the B. A. E., 31, pp. 463 - 576.

MÁRQUEZ, JUAN. *El gobernador cristiano, deducido de las vidas de Moysén y Josué, príncipes del pueblo de Dios.* Salamanca: Francisco de Cea Tesa, 1612. The author deduces principles of Christian government from the Bible.

MÁRTIR RIZO, JUAN PABLO. *Norte de príncipes y Vida de Rómulo.* Ed. José

Antonio Maravall. Madrid: Instituto de Estudios Políticos, 1945. In his guide to princes (1626), the author cites the best writers of Rome and modern Europe.

MAYÁNS Y SISCAR, GREGORIO. *Oración en alabanza de las eloquentissimas obras de Don Diego Saavedra Fajardo.* . . . Valencia: Antonio Bordazar, 1725. The frequently reprinted text of this pamphlet was written by a noted scholar of the eighteenth-century "republic of letters."

OROZCO Y COVARRUBIAS, JUAN DE. *Emblemas morales.* Segovia: Juan de la Cuesta, 1589. The author defines the emblem and produces an example of the genre.

QUEVEDO Y VILLEGAS, FRANCISCO DE. *Política de Dios, govierno de Christo.* Ed. James O. Crosby. Madrid: Editorial Castalia, 1966. The first part (1626) of this anti-Machiavellian treatise preceded *Idea de un príncipe* by fourteen years. The editor provides a model scholarly text.

RIBADENEYRA, PEDRO DE. *Tratado de la religión y virtudes que debe tener el príncipe cristiano para gobernar y conservar sus estados, contra lo que Nicolás Maquiavelo y los políticos deste tiempo enseñan.* Short title: *Tratado del príncipe cristiano.* In *Obras escogidas*, B. A. E., 60 , pp. 449 - 587. Madrid: M. Ribadeneyra, 1868. A significant treatise in the political literature of the age (1595).

SECONDARY SOURCES

1. *Books and Monographs*

Alonso-FUEYO, SABINO. *Saavedra Fajardo: El hombre y su filosofía.* Valencia: Editorial Guerri, 1949. A collection of articles that won the National Prize in Journalism.

BATAILLON, MARCEL. *Erasmo y España: estudios sobre la historia espiritual del siglo XVI.* Translated by Antonio Alatorre. 2 vols. Mexico/Buenos Aires: Fondo de Cultura Económica, 1959. Portrays the intellectual world from which seventeenth-century thinkers developed. The original edition is in French (1937).

BATES, MARGARET J. *"Discreción" in the Works of Cervantes: A Semantic Study.* Washington, D. C.: The Catholic University of America Press, 1945. The author documents distinctions in the meaning of concepts related to "prudence."

BLAIR, HUGH. *Lecciones sobre la retórica y las bellas letras por Hugo Blair.* Translated by José Luis Munárriz. 4 vols. Madrid: Antonio Cruzado, 1798 - 1800. The translator changed Blair's text, devoting Chapter 20 (II, 209 - 63) to Cervantes's style and Chapter 21 (II, 264 - 92) to a critique of Saavedra's style.

BOUGEANT, GUILLAUME HYACINTHE. *Histoire du traité de Westphalie ou des négotiations qui se firent à Münster et à Osnabrug pour établir la paix entre toutes les puissances de l'Europe.* 6 vols. Paris: Didot, 1751. Contains references to Saavedra from the French point of view.

CORTINES Y MURUBE, FELIPE. *Ideas jurídicas de Saavedra Fajardo*. Sevilla: Librería e Imprenta de Izquierdo y Compa., 1907. Deals with Saavedra's ideas on international, political, penal, administrative, economic, and civil law.

DOWLING, JOHN. *El pensamiento político-filosófico de Saavedra Fajardo: posturas del siglo XVII ante la decadencia y conservación de monarquías*. Murcia: Academia de Alfonso X el Sabio, 1957. Demonstrates Saavedra's position in the intellectual currents of his time.

ESSEN, ALFRED VAN DER. *Le Cardinal-Infant et la politique européene de l'Espagne, 1609 - 1641*. Brussels: Les Presses de Belgique, 1944. Deals with the role of Fernando, brother of Philip IV, in the European scene while Saavedra was active as a diplomat.

FRAGA IRIBARNE, MANUEL. *Don Diego de Saavedra Fajardo y la diplomacia de su época*. Madrid: Dirección General de Relaciones Culturales del Ministerio de Asuntos Exteriores, 1955. This excellent contribution to diplomatic history is based on extensive research in archives and contains new material never before published.

GALINO CARRILLO, MAÑA ÁNGELES. *Los tratados sobre educación de príncipes: siglos XVI y XVII*. Madrid: C. S. I. C., Instituto "San José de Calasanz" de Pedagogía, 1948. Deals with books on the upbringing of princes from the Middle Ages through the seventeenth century.

GREEN, OTIS H. *Spain and the Western Tradition: The Castilian Mind in Literature from El Cid to Calderón*. 4 vols. Madison, Milwaukee, and London: The University of Wisconsin Press, 1963 - 66. Presents the intellectual background of Spain and Europe and treats Saavedra specifically in Vol. IV, Chapter I.

GÜNTER, HEINRICH. *Die Habsburger Liga, 1625 - 1635: Briefe und Akten aus dem General-Archiv zu Simancas*. Berlin: Emil Ebering, 1908. The documents include correspondence sent to Saavedra in Germany.

HAFTER, MONROE Z. *Gracián and Perfection: Spanish Moralists of the Seventeenth Century*. Cambridge, Mass.: Harvard University Press, 1966. The book deals with Quevedo, Saavedra Fajardo, and Gracián. The chapter on Saavedra is excellent.

JOVER, JOSÉ MARIA. *1635: Historia de una polémica y semblanza de una generación*. Madrid: C. S. I. C., Instituto Jerónimo Zurita, 1949. Presents the Spanish position in the final phases of the Thirty Years' War. Chapter X is entitled "Saavedra Fajardo ante 1635."

LABROUSSE, ROGER. *Essai sur la philosophie politique de l'ancienne Espagne. Politique de la raison et politique de la foi*. Paris: Librairie de Recueil Sirey, 1938. Studies the conflict between practical politics and religious morality There is a Spanish version, *La doble herencia política de España*. Translated by Enrique Massaguer. Barcelona: Bosch, 1942.

MARAVALL, JOSÉ ANTONIO. *La teoría española del estado en el siglo XVII*. Madrid: Instituto de Estudios Políticos, 1944. This book is the point of departure for studies on seventeenth-century Spanish political literature. There is a French translation: *La philosophie politique espagnole au XVII siècle dans ses rapports avec l'esprit de la Contre-Réforme.* Translated by Louis Cazes and Pierre Mesnard. Paris: Librairie philosophique J. Vrin, 1955.

MURILLO FERROL, FRANCISCO. *Saavedra Fajardo y la política del barroco.* Madrid: Instituto de Estudios Políticos, 1957. Emphasizes Tacitism and Machiavellianism in Saavedra's work.

QUER Y BOULE, LUIS. *Apuntes hispano suizos.* Madrid: Espasa-Calpe 1931. Studies relations between Spain and Switzerland at various times in history.

_____. *La embajada de Saavedra Fajardo en Suiza: apuntes históricos, 1639 - 1642.* Madrid: Imprenta de Ramona Velasco, 1931. This monograph is devoted exclusively to Saavedra Fajardo's missions in Switzerland.

2. *Periodical Articles and Essays in Books*

ALDEA, QUINTIN. "Don Diego Saavedra Fajardo y la paz de Europa: dos documentos inéditos; en el tercer centenario de la Paz de los Pirineos, 1659 - 1959." *Humanidades* (Universidad Pontificia de Comillas) 9, No. 22 (1956): 103 - 24. Aldea describes and prints *Proposta fatta dal Sig. Don Diego Sciavedra alla Dieta de cantoni catolici in Lucerna* (1639), and the tract *Suspiros de Francia* (1643).

_____. "España, el Papado y el Imperio durante la Guerra de los Treinta Años. I. Instrucciones a los Embajadores de España en Roma (1631 - 1643)." *Miscelánea Comillas* 29 (1958): 291 - 437. Document No. 1 is "Instrucción de don Diego de Saavedra Fajardo al Marqués de Castel Rodrigo," pp. 303 - 315, written between April and October, 1631.

BAQUERO GOYANES, MARIANO. "El tema del gran teatro del mundo en las 'Empresas políticas' de Saavedra Fajardo." *Monteagudo* 1 (1953): 4 - 10. The author shows Saavedra's concept of the life of the prince as a theatrical performance.

BLEZNICK, DONALD W. "Spanish Reaction to Machiavelli in the Sixteenth and Seventeenth Centuries." *Journal of the History of Ideas* 19 (1958): 542 - 50. The author recognizes anti-Machiavellian currents but "aims to establish that Spaniards were far from being unanimously anti-Machiavellian . . ." (p. 542).

BONET, CARMELO M. "En torno al estilo de Saavedra Fajardo." *Boletín de la Academia Argentina de Letras* 9 (1941): 121 - 33. Emphasizes the significance of anecdote in producing clarity of style.

FRANK DE ANDREA, PETER. "Saavedra Fajardo y su visión del gobernante." *Cuadernos Americanos* Año 7, No. 42 (1948): 170 - 89. Places Saavedra's concept of the ruler in its historical setting.

GREEN, OTIS H. "Documentos y datos sobre la estancia de Saavedra Fajardo en Italia." *Bulletin Hispanique* 39 (1937): 367 - 74. Clarifies dates and incidents in Saavedra's long sojourn in Italy.

HAFTER, MONROE Z. "Deviousness in Saavedra Fajardo's *Idea de un príncipe.*" *The Romanic Review* 49 (1958): 161 - 67. Documents Saavedra's ambiguity with respect to Machiavellian practices.

————. "The Enlightenment's Interpretation of Saavedra Fajardo." *Hispanic Review* 41 (1973): 639 - 53. Traces the popularity of *Idea de un príncipe* and *República literaria* in the seventeenth and eighteenth centuries.

————. "Saavedra Fajardo plagiado en *El no importa de España* de Francisco Santos." *Bulletin Hispanique* 61 (1959): 5 - 11. Shows how Santos appropriated passages from *Idea de un príncipe* and adapted them for his own use.

MARAVALL, JOSÉ ANTONIO. "La corriente doctrinal del tacitismo político en España." *Cuadernos Hispanoamericanos*, Nos. 238 - 40 (1969), pp. 645 - 67. Compares writers who used the works of Tacitus to introduce Machiavellian ideas with others who combatted both Tacitus and Machiavelli.

————. "Moral de acomodación y carácter conflictivo de la libertad (Notas sobre Saavedra Fajardo)." *Cuadernos Hispanoamericanos* (Madrid), Nos. 257 - 58 (1971), pp. 663 - 93. A study of Saavedra's moral position on accommodation to circumstances.

MÁRQUEZ, JAVIER. "El mercantilismo de Saavedra Fajardo."*El Trimestre Económico* (Mexico) 10, No. 2 (1943): 247 - 86. A study of an aspect of Saavedra's work which interested eighteenth-century thinkers.

Because Azorín helped create the modern vogue for Saavedra Fajardo, I give in chronological order, from 1908 to 1949, all of his essays on Saavedra of which I know:

MARTINEZ RUIZ, JOSÉ [AZORIN]. "Saavedra Fajardo y la vulpeja" in *Obras completas* II, 391 - 92. Madrid: Aguilar, 1947 - 54. Chapter XIX of *El político* (1908).

————. "Saavedra Fajardo" in *Obras completas*, II, 551 - 55. *Lecturas españolas* (1912).

————. "La decadencia de España" in *Obras completas*, II, 753 - 57. *Clásicos y modernos* (1913).

————. "Pinturas viejas" in *Obras completas*, III, 914 - 32. *Entre España y Francia* (1917).

————. "Saavedra Fajardo" in *Obras completas*, IV, 313 - 40. *De Granada a Castelar* (1922).

————. "Saavedra Fajardo" in *Obras completas*, IX, 1337 - 40. *ABC*, Aug. 13, 1946.

————. "Saavedra Fajardo." *ABC*, Nov. 8, 1949.

MUÑOZ ALONSO, ALEJANDRO. "Revisión bibliográfica de Saavedra Fajardo." *Revista de Estudios Políticos*, No. 99 (1958), pp. 236 - 45. Evaluates works that appeared around the year 1948, the tercentenary of Saavedra's death.

PRAAG, J. A. VAN. "Apuntes bibliográficos sobre Saavedra Fajardo." *Boletín de la Real Academia Española* 16 (1929): 652 - 57. The author cites editions and translations that he found in libraries of the Low Countries.

RAMOS, JUAN P. "Don Diego de Saavedra Fajardo." *Boletín de la Academia Argentina de Letras* 9 (1941): 7 - 25. A eulogy in which the author contrasts Saavedra with Montaigne and compares him with Machiavelli.

SÁNCHEZ AGESTA, LUIS. "España y Europa en la crisis del siglo XVII (Raíz histórica de una actitud polémica)." *Revista de Estudios Políticos*, No. 91 (1957), pp. 55 - 76. A discussion of Vitoria, Mariana, Saavedra, and others on heresy, Machiavellianism, and universal monarchy.

SÁNCHEZ MORENO, JOSÉ. "Estimación del arte en la obra de Saavedra Fajardo." *Monteagudo* 7 (1954): 10 - 17. The author shows Saavedra's extensive use of the plastic arts.

SEMPERE Y GUARINOS, JUAN. *Biblioteca española económica-política.* 4 vols. Madrid: Imprenta de Sancha, 1801 - 21. In the chapter devoted to Saavedra (3 [1804], lxix - xix), Sempere usually approves Saavedra's economic ideas but criticizes his style.

SPINI, GIORGIO. "Uno scritto sconosciuto di Saavedra Fajardo." *Hispania. Revista Española de Historia* (Instituto Jerónimo Zurita) 2, No. 8 (1942): 438 - 51. The writer contends that Saavedra is the author of the tract *Indisposizione generale della monarchia di Spagna*, which he reprints.

TIERNO GALVAN, ENRIQUE. "Saavedra y Fajardo, teórico y ciudadano del Estado barroco." *Revista Española de Derecho Internacional* 1 (1948): 467 - 76. The author studies Saavedra as a man of faith who lived in a world that was changing from faith to reason.

URMENETA, FERMIN DE. "Sobre estética saavedriana," *Revista de Ideas Estéticas* 29 (1971): 59 - 69. The author interprets Saavedra's ideas on the visual arts, music, and poetry.

3. *Theses and Dissertations*

LUNDELIUS, MARGUERITE RUTH. "A Comparative Study of the *Vanity of the Arts and Sciences* by Henry Cornelius Agrippa and the *República literaria* by Diego de Saavedra Fajardo." M. A. thesis, University of Texas, 1954. Offers detailed proof of Saavedra's debt to the Agrippa book.

WOLFE, PHILLIP J. "Dialogue et société: Le genre du dialogue en France de 1630 à 1671." Ph.D. Dissertation, Princeton University, 1974. Provides the background for understanding the significance of Saavedra's dialogue *Locuras de Europa*.

Index

(Titles of works by Saavedra Fajardo are indexed under his name. Fictional names are marked with an asterisk.)

159